From Death to Destiny

Derrick Gates

From Death to Destiny
Derrick Gate ©2014

Roar Publications
Kansas City, Missouri

www.roarpublications.com

This book or parts thereof may not be reproduced in any form, stored in a retrieval system, or transmitted in any form by any means-electronic, mechanical, photocopy, recording, or otherwise - without prior written permission of the publisher/owner, except as provided by United States of America Copy right law.

Unless otherwise noted, all Scripture verses are from the New International Version, The Holy Bible ©1973, 1978, 1984 by International Bible Society

Used by permission of Zondervan Publishing House

ISBN-13: 978-1499335156

Endorsements

Pastor Derrick's Testimony "From Death to Destiny" is an amazing story showing God's Love, Mercy, and Grace. It shows how God never leaves us or forsakes us. It's Raw and Real. It's not your cookie cutter testimony and I Love the fact that it's not watered down like most testimonies you will read. He lays his life out and doesn't hold anything back. I love how it shows that people may give up us and have there opinions but the opinion that matters is God's and God never gives up on us. I really love that it shows when God calls and anoints us that what man thinks or does doesn't matter at all. Through Pastor Derricks book God shows that plans He has for your life will come to happen and nothing the devil throws at you will stop Him. "From Death to Destiny will set many people free and thousands upon thousands will come to find Jesus through this book.

Roger Hill Jr

This powerful book is a must-read for anyone who has felt like giving up on life or has felt less than valuable! If you have ever wondered, "why don't I feel loved? Why is my life such a mess? Is this all there is? There has to be more to life!" then keep reading. There is hope for you! Pastor Derrick has lived a life that many experience but only a few survive. He passionately relays his own life story from beginnings of desperation and depression to ultimate victory. Like so many of us, he searched for unconditional love, acceptance and approval in all of the wrong places. That fruitless search led him to the brink of death on more than one occasion. The lessons in his story are clear. You have a real enemy that seeks to destroy, abuse and discard you when he is finished with his sick, sadistic games. But you also have an amazingly powerful ally in God that can restore and elevate your life to a place of absolute joy, peace and fulfillment. That can be your reality if you surrender your broken life for His all-fulfilling one. You won't find a bunch of irrelevant religious gobbledygook here. This is real and raw. The underbelly of life exposed for what it truly is. An illusion, a counterfeit for the real, rewarding life we can have in relationship with our Heavenly Father.

Alessandro Sanford
Spirit Fire Ministries, Olathe, KS

Derrick Gates is one of Jesus' trophies of His accomplishments on the cross. Derricks story will inspire you and give you hope for your lost loved ones no matter how dark the situation. Derricks story is a beautiful display of Gods saving grace! I believe this book will set many free!

-Josh MacDonald
(Josh MacDonald is a national and international speaker and is also a leader at the International House of Prayer in Kansas City, MO.

Acknowledgements

First and foremost thank you, Jesus Christ, for shedding your blood at the cross to pay my many debts. I love you so very much and look forward to seeing you face to face someday.

Thank you to my wife Nena for your understanding, love, and support of my life and of the calling that God placed on me.

Thank you Mom you have always been a rock in my life. I love you so very much!

I thank you Pastor Honeycutt for being a great mentor and spiritual leader in my life.

I thank you Steve Bubbna for being a father figure when I didn't have one.

Thank you to all that have believed, sowed, and spoke into my life and ministry. I love you all very much.

Dedication

I write this book in hopes of inspiring people to change their lives –in hopes that some will reflect upon their own lives and see that there is something more out there for them. I want them to know that God wants the very best for all of us. I write this book especially for my children (Jesse, Savannah, and Derrick) that they learn from my mistakes and steer far from the road that I traveled. I love all three of you very much, and it would kill me to see you suffer the world the way I did. Also, to my only son, you are only 5 as I write this dedication. I hope that you will read this one day and know that being a man is not about how many women you've had, how much you can drink, how many dares you take, or how many fights you have won. It's about making good decisions and learning from the bad ones and truly loving yourself and Jesus

WARNING

Much prayer and fasting went into the writing of this book. This book was written to

(1) help the afflicted and show them the love of Christ, and

(2) to show the loved ones of the afflicted a small segment of the life and hope that they can achieve.

This book contains explicit and graphic details about sexual and drug abuse and may not be suitable for young readers. We suggest you pray that God gives you guidance in reading the story.

Table of Contents

Chapter 1: Bad Seed	1
Chapter 2: More of the Same Thing	5
Chapter 3: Dare to Shut Up	15
Chapter 4: Drug Addictions	21
Chapter 5: The Beatings	25
Chapter 6: Crash Bang Boom	33
Chapter 7: Powder	41
Chapter 8: Gang Life in a Small Town	45
Chapter 9: Finding Jesus	49
Chapter 10: Learning to Live Life	55
Chapter 11: Christian College	63
Chapter 12: When God and the Church Don't Want You	69
Chapter 13: A New Low	81
Chapter 14: Go Big or Go Home	101
Chapter 15: Checking Out	109

Table of Contents

Chapter 16: Jesus Encounter   113

Chapter 17 We Meet Again   115

Chapter 18: This Place Again   119

Chapter 19: Bags Packed   123

Chapter 20: God Catches Me   129

Chapter 21: City of Refuge   133

Chapter 22: Jam for the Lamb   135

Chapter 23: Preaching Machine   139

Chapter 24: Final Warning   143

Chapter 25: Nena   153

Chapter 26: Losing it All   159

Chapter 27: Fresh Start   171

Chapter 28: KC Here I Come   177

Chapter 29: Loud and Clear   183

How Do I Get Saved?   **191**

A Bad Seed

Sometimes walking the isle of the church and preaching reminds of my past, and sometimes when that memory hits, I wonder how I got to this place— how did I get from there to here? This is my story; this is how I conquered death and stepped into the destiny that God had for me. This is how I beat the devil.

It gets hot in southern Kansas – the humidity is what's the worst; its that kind of hot that just sticks to your skin and makes all your clothes cling to you. That's the kind of day it was – barely afternoon, and my father was strung out and drunk beyond compare. If you listen, you may be able to hear the repeated thuds of his knifes hitting the floor over and over, sticking into the pre-manufactured floor of a old 60's model single wide trailer. The woman begging him to stop is not one of his girl friends; it's my mother, the prettiest women in the county. She was going through a living Hell as he laughed and threw another knife, growling at her to dance. The baby screaming in the playpen in the corner, well, that was me as I watched my father toy with the idea of just killing my mother. Death was wanting, and when death wants you, he doesn't like to give up.

These were typical nights in my family as just a few nights later death would come wanting again. Death had taken up residence in my fathers mind. When my mother told him that she was pregnant, instead of a happy embrace with thoughts of the future, he tried to get rid of me by throwing my mother down the stairs and laughing about it.

Our typical redneck trailer set right on the opposite side of the drive way from my grandparents farm house. My grandfather, a short stocky man, was a pig farmer, and my grandma was the stereotypical country women with white hair that would always have a apron on, cooking chicken and dumplings or some other country dish. This arrangement would be the very thing that saved my life at such a young age.

My mother was so very worn out – the kind of tired that you get when you can sleep for days and still feel exhausted. She was not going to take one more punch, not one more slap, one more black eye, one more knife thrown at her feet, or one more insulting word spoken against her. This night, when he came in smelling like a cross between cheap perfume and jack Daniels whiskey, would be very different. He was standing there in his typical, jerk stance, pointing at her, cussing at her with chewing tobacco spit dribbling down his chin and a hint of cocaine on his nostril. My mother's hands were shaking but her eyes were glimmering with fire. Death had whispered into her ear

A Bad Seed

now. Death was insistent that he would have someone's life in that trailer. In the shaking hands of my mother's was a shotgun pointed right at my fathers head. Strangely enough, his attitude didn't change at all. His face flushed red with anger with the vein in his neck thumping almost like the sound of the knifes hitting the floor a few days ago he scolded her. "You will never do it you stupid bitch – you don't have it in you." As a tear squeezed out of her eye she began to squeeze the trigger to the 20 gauge. "Robin, you don't want to do this" carried through the room in a soft firm voice. It was my grandfather, Calvin. He was creeping up the stairs to the wide-open trailer door. My mother now in complete sobbing state with her lips quivering squeaks out "yes I do!" "What about Derrick? Do you want to leave your son behind? Do you want to spend your life in prison and never see him again?" Now the sweat was dripping from every face in the room. A concerned face on grandpa, a look of confusion on mom, and the same smirk on my fathers face. In one built up moment, my mother collapses to the ground in a huddled mass, crying in her hands as my grandpa pushed by my father, giving him a look. He then knelt and held my mother tight.

I was two when this happened and that was the last time I would see my dad until I turned twenty-three.

From Death to Destiny

More of the Same Thing

After much anger, grieving, and many tears, my mother moved to town to try to start her life over. My father was her second marriage already, and so far she was not that great at picking the winner types.

A year or so had passed by, and my mother and I moved into a rental house that my grandfather owned in Garnett, Kansas. It was a small house, but it was good for us. Mom started to date again. The only one I remember was a man named Dan. The only two things I remember about him was that he had a really cool car (I think it was a red and black Dodge Charger), and his parents had a awesome lava lamp and a wooden paddle with holes in it. Ouch! It wasn't very long before my mother and Dan where engaged to get married. My mom was happy again. I loved to see her happy, and she sure was.

That happiness was short lived because the week of the wedding my mother walked in on her love, Dan, sleeping with one of her girlfriends. This was a pivotal point in my life because it is the first time I was directly involved in a altercation. Dan showed up to the house to get all of his personal belongings, and my mother was fuming, boiling over mad and instructed me to not let him out. So, I stood in front of the door and wouldn't let him through. I couldn't have been more than three or four, and I'm sure I was not threatening at all. It's almost humorous to think that I could stand there like that. I watched my mom fall onto the coach that night and cry her eyes out. Unfortunately, that would be a pattern in her life, a lot of tears and a lot of pain.

After another disappointment, my mother dropped me off at my grandparents for a while. She was working full time to support me and couldn't afford to pay for child care. I'm not sure how long it was. At my age, it seemed like six months or more. What I do know is that when she returned to get me she had another man tagging along with her.

Mom sat down at grandmas table, put me on her lap, held me tight, and whispered into my ear that she had someone special that she wanted me to meet. I think I can remember my grandma rolling her eyes when in walked a man in his early twenties with long braided hair and a typical 70's to early 80's style blue bandana rolled tight and rapped around his forehead. As he stuck his hand out to introduce himself, he said, "Hello, my name is David." I was a very shy little boy, and I just buried my face into my mother's neck.

Mom met David at a bar called "The Swamp". The Swamp was a biker dive with every shady character in town taking part in the activities there. David's best friend, Mike, owned the bar and held many dances. David was somewhere between a hippie and a biker. He loved bikes and hot rods, but the coolest thing to me was that he was a musician. You name it, and it seemed like he played it. I was fascinated with the guitar and music all together. David was great, and I really fell in love with him. Life seemed to be great –kind of a white trash fairy-tale.

David had started to be the father figure to me that I never had, but always desperately wanted. Not only did I have a dad for the first time, but I also had new grandparents that where awesome, aunts and uncles that where great to me, and cousins that fit like a glove.

One summer day, David took me fishing on his parents farm in rural Kansas near Osawatomie (Osawatomie is famous for John Brown, the iconic Abolitionist). Fishing then and even still is not my forte, but do you remember those little snoopy cartoon fishing poles? That's what I was fishing with that day. David always insisted that everyone use purple plastic worms. He carefully helped me thread my dark purple plastic worm onto the sharp hook, and then helped me cast my line in. With his help, I cast the line way into the water. After several minutes of watching the water, David took advantage of the opportunity to ask me a life altering question. "Buddy," he said, "how would you like to be my son?" I didn't understand what he meant. He then said, "I was thinking of adopting you— then your name would be Gates". I would often sit on the front porch and watch the neighbors' dads play and teach their sons to ride bikes, and I really wanted that. I really didn't understand. All I knew was that this was the dad that I had always wanted in my life. I just smiled, and about that time, my bober began to pop up and down in the pond water. I was so excited; I was trying to real it in, but it was too much. So, David helped. After a twenty-minute struggle, we had a cat fish that was as tall as I was. It was so cool having that huge fish and a dad sitting on the bank with me.

It wasn't long after that day that my mom and David tied the knot; it was a nice wedding with a lot of people. My mother looked so beautiful in her long white dress and I must say I looked pretty dang pimp in my tuxedo. I could have worn that tux every day; I thought I was the cats pajamas.

A month later mom, David and myself walked into the judge's chambers at the courthouse. The judge sat behind this huge oak desk and peered over his glasses, down his long nose at the paper-

More of the Same Thing

work in front of him. "Now Derrick," the Judge said and paused, "do you want David to be your daddy?" Then, he turned and looked down that long nose at me. With no hesitation, I squeaked out yes. And, that was it; I walked into the chambers Derrick Dee Badders and walked out Derrick Rollin Gates.

Not only did I get a family that day, but I also got a little brother the same year. Brandon was born and he had the chubbiest cheeks ever. Everyone always wanted to pinch his little cheeks.

It wasn't long before I noticed things starting to change in our new happy home. Maybe it was always there, and I was just getting old enough to recognize it. I really don't know. My parents were smoking so much pot that you would think it was a Cheech and Chong movie. David would come home later and later, drunker and drunker completely stoned out of his mind. They started fighting; it started as some small bickering back and forth on a regular basis and grew from there into shattered vases and bruised faces. They would scream so loud at each other that the whole block could hear them fighting. Back then nobody called the cops; it was the common practice to stay in your own business and act like you don't know anything. Eventually David started staying out throughout the night, and when we would see him, he was so high he couldn't even keep his eyes open.

Around the time that I turned eight years old David started to actively involve me in his addiction. "Get my tray!" he would bark. So, I would lay down on the floor and slide my hand under the couch to pull out the large orange and black pot tray. I think the tray had a picture of the Zig-Zag man on it, and was divided up into sections. You had your classic baggy rolled up with some stinky, skunk weed. Another section has a small pipe, scissors, the classic roach clip with the colored feathers attached, and some orange Zig-Zags because white Zig-Zags would have been unacceptable. The next section was seeds and stems that had been carefully processed from the weed. The last section was the freshly pruned, systemically cut marijuana. I would sit next to David and watch him in amazement as he prepared his pot like a doctor going into surgery.

The thing you have to understand about potheads is that everyone takes pride in their paraphernalia. I remember one of my parents' friends had a old sonic drive in window tray as their pot tray. Some are joint smokers, some would rather pack a bowl, and then you have the bong smokers; and they are a kind of like the weed smoking Olympians.

More of the Same Thing

My parents started leaving me with a couple of young girls that where four or five years older than I was. Their parents where friends with my parents, so it fell into place that they would be my baby sitters. One Friday night in Casey's bedroom, my life would forever change. Casey, Dana and I where sitting in the bedroom when Casey's older brother Brant walked in. I'm guessing that Brant was probably 16 or 17 at the time. He started to touch Dana and Casey's breasts and then slid his pants off. Over the next several minutes, he coerced both of them to touch his penis. Before I knew it both girls where giving him oral sex. I felt extremely uncomfortable to say the least, and did not want to be there in that room. Brant turned his attention to me, and he came over and pulled down my pants. As he fondled my private parts, both girls were instructed to rub themselves on me. Brant was so demanding, and I was so scared to say no. Before I knew it, he had me in full blown intercourse with both girls. The whole time he was instructing us what to do as he continued to fondle my body inside and out. Over the next year, I was molested and raped repeatedly in front of Brant and his friends, while my parents where typically a couple of rooms away. Some times they would come to my house, and like clock work they would tell my parents they were taking me for a walk; and of course my parents were all to glad to get rid of me. They would take me to the abandoned house next door and rape me in between the house and the tree row. I can't explain what this has done to my thinking through the years. It was a nightmare that haunted me for many years.

My grandpa Turner, my mom's dad, passed away. It was a strange night since it was the first time I was faced with someone who actually died. I was numb about it at first then a few hours later, I started to laugh and couldn't stop laughing. I'm not sure why I reacted like that. Later that night my grandma just rocked me back and forth on her lap as she told me how much my grandpa loved me. Within a few months my grandma moved out of state with my uncle, so we moved back to the farm right back to where all the death had try to creep in on me as a baby. Things continued to get so much worse.

More of the Same Thing

Dare to Shut Up

Out in the country, David was free to grow his own pot and do so much more. People would come and go like a McDonald's drive through to pick up there order. I started to see more than pot passing hands. They started selling white crosses, black beauties and crank that my dad's biker friends would bring in. David started using a lot of the speed and would become more and more paranoid by the day. I was nine years old and he would walk by starring at me asking me, "Who are you talking to?" He would look at me with this evil look and say, "You better not be snitching you little mother fucker!" I would say, "I'm not talking to anyone." I didn't even know what snitching was. He would slap me across the mouth, punch me in the back of my head and pull my hair until it would come out. This is when my fear for him moved to another level. I was really getting scared, but it wasn't the normal scared it was the kind where I would just hide in a corner and my lips and hands would tremble, the kind where you just weren't sure if you where going to wake up the next day. This was the kind of scared that made you wonder what did I do to deserve this. I would lay in bed and think, "what do I do, what do I say and who would I say it too?" Since I didn't have anyone. I didn't say anything I just sucked it up and went another day after day after day.

The problem I had with this whole thing was that I would go to school and listen to all the teachers, D.A.R.E, Nancy Reagan and McGruff the crime dog tell me that drugs were wrong and that you should tell on people that do drugs. Then you go home to your mom and dad smoking joint after joint, line after line and pill after pill. I wanted to tell, I wanted to be free of all the guilt that I had everyday going to school. But, if I tattle tell, I will never see my mother again. So, you just close your eyes and try to ignore it, but ignoring it had become impossible.

The life style of my parents was starting to affect me mentally. I was just so sad all the time, so tired, so lost and so confused. I would get so angry at myself for being alive that I started to become fascinated and day dream about killing myself. Death was finally warming his way into my thought processes. How could I kill myself? I would lay awake at night listening to the cars come and go out of my parents drive way, listening to them fight and scream, throwing pictures and glasses at each other then listen to the sounds of them having sex after all of it. The whole time wondering how could I just leave? Not leave the house but leave my life. Watching TV, I had learned about guns, but I didn't have one and didn't know where David kept his. I learned about hanging, but I didn't have a clue how to tie a noose at nine. I tried to hang myself with shoe laces, but the shoe laces just broke. I thought about over dosing on pills, but good luck trying to get pills from drug addicts. Then I remembered the razor. The razor was the best way for a young boy like me. It was easy to get and easy to hide. I could find plenty around a house of drug addicts. So, razor it was.

The thing about a razor is that you build a relationship with the sharp metal blade. The way it would slice through your skin – you didn't feel the pain until the razor slid in and out of the skin. What I found out was that the pain made me feel good. As I warmed my way up to letting death have his way with me, I practiced by cutting my body. I started to feel alive. With the pain came freedom to know that I was still alive. The blade was becoming my friend, my family and my savior. This savior was a counterfeit because the only thing this savior wanted was my dead body on a hard, cold slab. The blade was only getting to know me, so when I least expected it he would hand me over to the clutches of death.

I would cut my body over and over sometimes toying dangerously close to my veins. It was almost a high in itself to watch myself come so close to death then back the razor off just short of a vein. The blood dripping from my arms made me feel alive.

In a world that I felt so lost in, the blade was my only friend.

The level of addiction was constantly on the rise; with the bar being raised on addiction came an equal raise in the arena of mental torment. Thinking back, this was the time when my addiction first surfaced. They had an addiction to drugs, and I had an addiction to pain.

The mental abuse from David started pretty subtle. He was just so very abrasive to me; I never did anything right –it was clear that he thought I was a chronic screw up. Then he turned it up a notch. We would whisper in my ear things like, "You will never be anything", "I wish you where dead", "Your own mother hates you", "You're a fucking looser", "I fucking hate you, you stupid mother fucker", "Your a fucking fat waste of space" and so much more. You know, after you hear these things over and over for years, you start to believe them. It is amazing what the power of the spoken word has over the people in your life. As the verbal mental abuse continued, I started to plummet deeper and deeper into depression. As the depression worsened, my behavior became stranger. I had no friends, the only people I really had around were the adults that where partying with my parents. So many times people would stay the weekends and sometimes longer.

I remember biker Mike, one of David's friends, he always had on jeans, a black pocket t-shirt with a pack of smokes hanging out, and a big smith hat. He would stay every now and then typically having a different woman with him each time he came. He would stay in the room next to mine, and I would watch him do drugs then have sex with the flavor of the night.

From everything I could tell at that age, drugs made you happy apparently, violence was normal, and perversion was natural. My mother would talk about how unhappy she was all the time, and David would just gripe and gripe. It would always end with drugs. This seemed to change the mood for them, so naturally I thought it would change the mood for me.

From Death to Destiny

CHAPTER FOUR
DRUG ADDICTION

Drug Addiction

Colony is a very small town in rural southeast Kansas. It has no particular claim to fame; nothing spectacular has ever happened there that I have ever known about, but it happened to be 6 miles from the farm I lived on and where my cousin lived.

One Saturday morning I was at my cousin's house with nothing really planned to do. It was always strange at my cousins. We would do things like order pizzas and have them sent to people or book airline tickets under other peoples names. Sometimes he would root around in his mother's room and find porn to watch. I always thought it a tad bit bizarre to watch porn of your mother, but then again I watched it, and it was of my aunt. This day was different for me because of one strange older man that came by the house. This guy had a long scraggly beard and beady eyes setting behind small glasses; he was eccentric in his movements and language, and he rode an old Honda Gold Wing Motorcycle and the side compartments where packed full of porn magazines.

Looking back, the fact that he was a 35 year old man looking at porn and hanging out with nine and thirteen year old boys should have been a huge red flag. That day, he pulled out a bag of weed (remember I knew a lot about weed). I had been rolling joints and packing bowls for a year now; the thing was that I never smoked it. That day I decided to get rid of my sadness, my desperation and my depression. My cousin and the bearded fellow put the pot on an aluminum Pepsi can they had made into a pipe. I had the privilege since it was my first time to take the first toke. So, I put the can up to my lips and my cousin lite the pot in a circular motion. I took a long drag sucking in this thick harsh smoke, and then, uncontrollably I started to cough blowing all the pot off the Pepsi can and all over the floor. My cousin screams out "Damn it! Party foul!". Unbelievably I was high already and off to the races. The high was intense for someone with virgin lungs. My head felt clouded and loopy my body felt light like I could float. It was great.

    I had a great advantage than most people because David grew his own weed to sell. I would always steal it from all the different places he hid it. At times he would have so much weed that he didn't even know where he put all of it. Our barn had a complete growing operation; we would have starter plants inside with grow lights, and then transfer them outside under military camouflage tents once they hit a certain age. When it was time to harvest, they would come back into the barn and put onto big screens with fans on them to dry. He wasn't a king pin or anything, but he definitely had some weed going on.

Drug Addiction

Smoking weed was great for me for several reasons. Number one, I felt an escape from the crappy life that I had been dealt. Number two, my parents smoked so much that they couldn't smell or tell when I was smoking. Number three, David had so much weed around that he never knew when I took it or not, or maybe he did and just never said anything about it.

From Death to Destiny

CHAPTER FIVE
THE BEATINGS

The Beatings

It wasn't long before the demons inside David started to grow and stretch him from the boundaries of mental and verbal abuse to the foundations of good old fashioned beatings. It started with the occasional slap across my mothers face when mom would confront him about his all night escapades with other women. He would come home reeking of stimey, meth smoke, beer and sleazy sex. His hair was in disarray, something crossed between Einstein and the band A Flock of Seagulls, his clothes half on, and he had hickies all over his body – a blatant disrespect for my mother. I remember the rage that would ripple through my body when I would hear his calloused, motor-grease-stained hand make contact with my mother's soft face. Then, he would perform his ritualistic dance through the house, breaking glass, throwing chairs and seeing who could scream the loudest. I can still feel the anxious, nervous energy that would well up inside as I would fantasize of the things I would do to him if only I was a little bigger. I would visualize tying him down and strapping his filthy smelly hands into his mouth until he choked on his own vomit from his gag reflex, all the while I would sit and watch asking him if it was worth every time he touched my mother body with filthy cheating hands. It really didn't take much to see that the devil inside David was quickly becoming the devil inside me.

Slowly the beatings would shift from my mother to me. I would seriously doubt that he would even remember all the paranoid fits he would throw as the abuse went from spanking to fists and from fists to 2X4's, golf clubs, broom handles or what ever may be within his grasp. He loved to take me to the garage and throw me to the ground, kneel over me screech in my ear how worthless I was and that I would never be anything.

In the beginning, I didn't speak much about the abuse because I didn't want it any worse for my mother than it already was. The only thing I could do to protect her was to channel some of the violence onto me, but the sad reality was the demons within David had plenty of abuse to go around.

David's behavior became so haunting that it would rival any Hollywood movie. My room was on the second floor of our farm house and on many occasions, I would be sitting at my desk doing homework or drawing, and I would notice him in the reflection of my mirror perched outside my bedroom window peering in at me with his demonic, beady eyes. In case you have never unexpectedly caught a glimpse of someone looking in a window at you, I will explain to you that it is very scary and unnerving; it literally sends a shock wave through your body and you begin to quiver in fear and adrenalin flows through your veins. Several times when he noticed that had caught him looking at me, he would slide in through the window and give me a beating for looking at him. He would scream, "Don't you fucking look at me you little son of a bitch! Never look at me!" I have no idea why he would do this creepy, pysco behavior except that he was under the influence of drugs and the demons.

This was also the age that I first ever looked at a picture of Jesus and to be perfectly honest I was frightened by the picture of him. I can't tell you why it spooked me, but it really did. Maybe it was the peering eyes. You know how they follow you no matter where you walk—so creepy. I didn't know the first thing about God back then. It wasn't anything anyone in my home would ever speak of for sure. I had not ever set foot in a church that I could remember outside of the occasional wedding or funeral. I laid on my bed that night wondering if there was really a God, and if there was a God, why did I have to live this way? Why would God let things like this happen to a little boy and his mom? I didn't hear God answer me that night, so I just assumed that if there was a God, which I highly doubted, but if there was, he didn't want anything to do with a worthless kid like me that would never be anything. I even remember reasoning with myself thinking that I understand why he wouldn't want me. I didn't have anything to offer Him.

Beating after beating continued. It felt like a train that was accelerating out of control. I recall being at school and sitting on one butt cheek or the other because I was so bruised I couldn't stand it. Or my back being so swollen, I couldn't set back on the bus seats. My mother was working the overnight shift at a nursing home and it gave David ample opportunity to party. When the cats' away, the mice will play! David would be so high and strung out on dope, coke or whatever combination of drugs, that he would chain me up in the garage. In some respects, it was better because typically if it was a chain day, then I wouldn't get beat as bad. To this day, I still get a little queasy to my stomach when I look at chains.

One day I was called into the school counselor's office where they where asking me questions about my home life, and I was petrified to answer. I didn't want to talk about the nightmare that I had been living in every day. Besides, I had it drilled into me for years now that what happens at home stays at home, and that snitches get stitches. They kept prying and prying at me wanting information about whether I was abused and information on all the who's, how's, why's and where's of the entire circle of confusing chaos.

With sweat beading down my cheeks, faced

The Beatings

with the CIA style interrogation of the school, Gestapo counseling regime, I finally broke and told them that I wanted to kill myself and that was it. I didn't say anything about David, the beatings, the drugs or anything, I didn't even want to say anything because it would break the air tight family motto, and I didn't want anymore drama in my life than what I already had. The counselors then chose to go ahead and call my parents and visit with them about my depression and suicidal thoughts.

It seemed that my parents let conversation roll off there shoulders. I don't know maybe they where more concerned behind closed doors. At any rate, nothing changed. The beatings continued and got more severe. I would try to keep my head up but it was very hard. The only thing that I really wanted was to die.

One day I decided I was going to get back at David. I went back behind the old barn where he had his growing operation of marijuana plants. The plants were about knee high and all neatly in rows with straw up around the base and a sprinkler system along each row. There was about sixty plants if I remember correctly, and I went on a rampage. I up rooted every single plant and broke the stocks off from the roots then poured bleach in every hole that they had been in. Then, I went into the back room of the barn where he had his drying operation and poured bleach all over all of his pot that was drying and being prepared for bagging.

It felt so good and liberating to do that and he never said a word to me about it. He made so many enemies that I'm sure he thought it was some one giving him some payback.

The Beatings

CHAPTER SIX
CRASH BANG BOOM

Crash, Bang, Boom

When I was eleven years old, my mother, brother and myself were on the way to fifth-grade enrollment in a predominately Amish and Mennonite school that I attended in the rural Kansas town called Westphalia. In my class, I had eleven other students: eight girls and three boys me being one of them. The road to the school was through the country on old gravel roads. Typically on these roads, you can see the dust clouds from far away of cars coming or going. This particular morning was different because it had rained a small amount: therefore, wetting the dust rendering it incapable of taking flight. Another thing about driving in the country is that you don't have a city worker out keeping the corners nice and manicured. As we passed though the intersection, a truck pulling a trailer blew through the stop sign and my mother t-boned the truck, and the trailer wrapped our car up then spun us down the road like a old string top and then spun us back out ending with our car wrapped around a telephone pole.

It was dizzying how fast everything happened. One minute your talking and your brother won't shut up about a dumb toy that he has. Then, the next minute the horn was blowing constantly, blood was squirting everywhere and my mothers head laid against the steering wheel with her eyes rolled back into her head. Everything was in slow motion, and at the same time, my senses where at a peak from all of the adrenaline. It seemed like a hour—Brandon crying at the top of his lungs, the hiss of the radiator, and the smell of gas invading my nose. Then I shook my head as if to fling off the fog. Now that the fog was gone my adrenaline was pumping though my veins in a way I didn't know was possible. I flung the door open to get out and as I did, I felt something tugging at my leg. I looked down to see that part of the motor of the car had come through the dash and severed my leg. My flesh was intertwined in the metal from the car. I had to pull my entangled leg and rip my flesh from the bone to get out. I remember the feeling of muscle ripping out of my leg and even pulling from the back of my calf. I then pulled myself out of the completely mangled car and tried to stand. As soon as I took a step, blood began to run like a river down my leg and from various other parts of my body. The next step more of my flesh fell from my wounds on to the dirty gravel road. I then hobbled over to the driver side of the car and drug my mother and brother out. My mother was unconscious and had blood covering her face. My brother was completely unscathed. Then I ran to the truck. The Man driving somehow had his foot hyper-extended from his leg, and it was wrapped around the brake peddle with just his skin. I had to unwrap his foot to get him out. This being the day before cell phones where commonplace, I had no choice but to walk for help. I was bleeding a tremendous amount from my wounds, so I did what I had learned in boy scouts. I took off my blue and yellow Westphalia wolverine's shirt and wrapped it around my leg cutting off the blood supply. I noticed two houses each one being about a mile away both in different directions, so I just chose one and began to jog the best I could. I had lost so much blood that i was becoming so week as I got close to the house I started to notice that the house looked very abandoned. I walked to the porch and could see through the windows that the house was vacant. I collapsed on the porch in frustration, pain and weakness. As I laid there, I heard a very familiar sound. Off in a field was a tractor cutting hay in the meadow. I pulled myself up and headed to the field. Barely getting through the fence, I staggered through the field. Every step I took, the seeds and sticks from the weeds would scrape through my open flesh. Every step I took, blood would slosh out of my shoe like I had walked through a river of blood. With each step I would take, the tractor seemed to be getting farther away. My vision started to get shaky, and my thoughts where coming and going. Finally, I was close enough to flag the farmer down, and within 30 minutes I was sitting on a couch in his house waiting on the ambulance. I was going into shock so they kept shoveling liquid into me and covering me in blankets. The small town hospital didn't think they could save my leg, so they rushed me a hour and a half to Kansas City to a hospital there. After a long trip to the City slipping in and out of consciousness, I finally got to the emergency room. They took me to surgery, and after a two-hour battle, I woke in recovery not sure what to think or expect, and I really wasn't ready for the insane amount of pain I was about to endure.

Days seemed like months and months seemed like years. It felt like I spent three or four years in that hospital waiting for the doctors to decide whether I would walk again. Some doctors even considered just cutting my leg off. None of it really mattered to me because I was getting real used to the morphine and codeine that they where pumping into me every second of the day. It was on my command basically! Press the button and ask for drugs a few minutes later, the nurse comes in with a shot. I was eleven and addicted.

After several months of laying around high and weeks of learning to walk again, I was released to go home, but was confined to a bed still not really being able to walk without a walker. I would just lay around all day and night watching movies. The only thing that changed at home was while I was laid up, David didn't beat me as much. I laid around for weeks trying to walk but couldn't with out the walker to assist me. They had moved a bed to the living room for me since I couldn't go up and down stairs. One particular night that I remember was when I was desperately needing to use the restroom, and I kept calling for help; but the party in the other room was too loud and out of control. So, I had to drag myself across the room pull myself up to the walker then I came out to the party. All the heads turned as my eyes instantly gazed on the long wall size mirror laid out on the table with lines of powder strown all over (out of site out of mind). As soon as I was gone, the party started back up. Soon after that day, my mom and David got into a big knock-down-drag-out fight, and she got into the car to leave. I was so scared of being left alone with David that I threw the walker down and started running the best I could out the door and to the car. When I was running, I felt a pop in my leg and a sharp pain and I fell to the ground. When they got me inside and took off the brace, they found blood draining down my leg. The scar had popped back open and I again had a open wound.

The doctors said they couldn't stitch or staple it, so they would have to treat it and try to heal it while it was a open wound. Everyday I would have to go to a rehabilitation specialist to treat the wound.

They would sit me in a whirlpool of hot water and iodine. They battled it and battled it, and I was getting worse and worse. I was becoming sick and soon the wound started to smell. One day the infection had gotten so bad that they rushed me back to Kansas city to find out that I had a very serious infection called gangrene.

Turned out, I had gangrene infection, the worst infection you can get. It was entering my blood stream, which would explain why I was so sick. The doctors spent ours cutting rotten flesh and puss away from my leg, and then they took skin from my upper leg and grafted it to my lower leg. After all of this battle, I didn't die, and I was even able to use my leg pretty good; however, my addiction to pain medication was raging at eleven. I would sneak pain pills and drink liquid morphine. I felt great when I was high; I didn't even worry about the beatings or the mental abuse. When I was high, I would just lay around all day and sleep or daydream.

Crash, Bang, Boom

From Death to Destiny

Powder

With snowdrifts waist high and what seemed to be polar temperatures, I was freaking out not being able to make it to town. I had run out of pain pills, and the pot was gone. I snooped around the house trying to find a roach or something to take the edge away and stumbled upon a small corner of a zip lock bag that was cut and sealed with the burn of a lighter. I knew that what was inside was not something I had ever done.

I had seen my parents and their friends toy with this many times, so it wasn't something that I was a complete stranger to. I sat on the corner of my bed and flirted back and forth with the thought of consuming this powder. Now I didn't have a real good concept of what each different powder would do, but I was pretty sure that it would take away the edge that I had. I decided to go for it. I opened the bag and poured the contents out into a pile on the table then I took a pinch of it put it to my nose and snorted as hard as I could.

Now I'm not exactly sure what I shoved into my nostrils that day, but I'm pretty sure it was Meth because within a half hour, I was cleaning my room, doing the dishes, and drawing pictures. I remember thinking, how bad can this be? All you do is clean. So now at twelve years old, I'm stealing dope from my father. It wasn't long before I was swiping a gram every couple of days. David would be so mad that he couldn't find his stuff, and I would think it was so funny. It was like my little way of getting back at him for being such a monster.

Powder

CHAPTER EIGHT
GANG LIFE IN A SMALL TOWN

Gang Life in a Small Town

I never understood those people who wanted to move to the country; I always felt that life in the boondocks was so dreadfully boring, and many times you would find trouble just to feel alive. We would do all kinds of things to break up the boredom: Super glue the door locks to the High School closed, egg the cop cars, sneak out with my friends Brian, Ilea and others to name a few. We would sneak out in the middle of the night and meet on old dirt roads just to hang out. The reality is that I wouldn't even have to sneak out—I just walked out.

By the time I was a sophomore in High school, I always had friends and I was a pretty popular guy. I was on the football team and had my share of dating girls, but something was always missing. I always felt like I had something to prove to my self and everyone else around. I was pretty good at hiding my drug use from others. There were only a couple of people in high school that knew that I did drugs, and they were getting their drugs from me. A couple of twin girls moved to town. Roni and Nita... they were real cool and I got along with them immediately. I kinda had a thing for Nita, even though she was pregnant. Unfortunately for me, she was pregnant by this Hispanic gang member from Kansas City. Phillip was a pretty cool cat, and in reality, I kinda looked up to him because he had the bad boy persona: he smoked, carried a gun, slept with women and acted like a bad boy.

He was a member of the NHC. It's what they call a set or a division of the CRIPS. The CRIPS are an international street gang that was founded in the early eighties in Orange County California. CRIP stands for Community Revitalization in Progress. The more Phillip and I hung out, the more I started to imitate him. I started to line my identity up with the gang mentality.

After about four months of hanging out with Phillip, I started meeting others in the gang, and it wasn't long before I was taking trips to Kansas City to get weed from some of these connections. One day Phillip asked me if I wanted to be family. Being family is something that means you will be a part of the gang. It would take me from being a friend of Phillips to being a friend of everyone's in the gang. So, I accepted mostly because the thought of having a different family sparked my interest. Phillip took me to a place in West Port Kansas City on a weekend. There we met with around twenty CRIPS that were office holders. Office holders meant that they where set in place similar to generals, majors and so on. And then you have your foot soldiers. The head of the set is called an OG, which means original gangster. The

Gang Life in a Small Town

guys circled around me and went to work on me. The idea is that I had to take a beating for three minutes with out falling each time you fall you get twenty seconds added on. Three minutes may not sound like a lot but let me tell you it's a long, long time to get punched and kicked over and over. I took a beating of a lifetime there, but after it was all said and done I was officially a CRIP.

We brought a lot of pot and cocaine down to the country towns. I put a little bit of cash in my pocket, got high for free, but most of all I liked being part of something that was bigger than me. Looking back, everything that happened in that season was so small. The Click that Phillip introduced me to was so small-time, and in reality, it was just a bunch of kids trying to be something they weren't. I even think that I learned later that Phillip was never a hardened street thug at all. He was a suburban kid trying to be cool just like I was a country kid trying to be cool. That's how things work, huh.

It amazing that this whole time I was able to stay in school. Some people knew and a lot of people speculated that I was in a gang. Most people just didn't ask because gang or not they knew I would thrash them.

From Death to Destiny

Finding Jesus

All my life I found pictures of Jesus a little creepy I didn't want to look at them. This long solemn faced white man with some hippie hair, he looked like some one that would be hanging out partying with my folks. Church just wasn't for me. As a matter of fact, I didn't even believe in God. I thought it was a little ridiculous that people believed in something so ludicrous. I went to church from time to time with friends, but that was it. Late in my sophomore year of high school, I had become best friends with a guy named Matt McGhee. Matt got me started going to the youth group in our town. We had three churches and one youth group. I knew the pastor of the community church, Steve Bubna, who was also the youth leader from school. He was a substitute teacher. Anyway, I started going to the youth group but I rationalized it with the fact that there where girls there.

I found something with Matt that I had never found before, and that was a true friend. I could tell Matt anything. Matt and I were inseparable. Matt never judged me no matter what it was that I was doing wrong; he always loved me anyway. To this day Matt is still one of my best friends. Although we don't see each other much, he is still part of my family.

I went to that youth group for about six months before I started attending the Colony Community Church. I would party at night and go to church during the day. Matt and I were there every Sunday and did things for the church, including singing songs. We also hung out at the pastor Steve's house, and I really started to like it. Actually, I was beginning to love it.

One day they announced that the youth would be taking a trip to Kansas City to see some Christian Contemporary artist named Carmen. I had no idea who Carmen was at all, and to be honest, I had zero desire to go or to listen to anything that was said. However, there was a girl named Beth that I was seeing that was a Christian and was really pushing hard for me to clean up my act, so between her and Matt they finally convinced me to go. We loaded up on a Saturday afternoon and took the two-hour trip to Kansas City. Six mini vans deep, we caravanned there. I still wasn't that excited about Carmen, but I was excited about getting out of town, but a little annoyed that I would not be back in time to get drunk. We pulled up to Kemper Arena, and there were cars as far as you could see. Thousands of people showed up to this free concert; it was really something to see. I can't remember how many people that place holds, but I'm pretty sure it is over twenty thousand, and I do know that they had to turn several thousand people away because they ran out of room. Carman's music these days isn't really my thing, but back then I thought it was pretty cool for Christian music. I thought Christian music was just like "The Old Rugged Cross" or "In the Garden" type of hymns. Carmen had it going on! The base was so hard that it would rumble my chest cavity, and he had back up hip hop dancers, basically anything you would find at a secular concert.

Then, at the end Carmen stopped everything and gave a alter call. I had never seen a alter call before. The little community church never gave alter calls back then. Carmen talked about accepting Jesus into your heart, and I had never heard that before. I know that my spirit cried out to God's in that moment, and when Carmen invited people to come and pray, all my pride all my "I'm a man and I don't need anybody" left and all I knew is that I had to get to Him so I could learn how to have this in my life. We were way up in the nose bleed section, and I jumped and hopped every bar and every barrier, knocked people out of the way and even jumped one level to make sure that I got what I was hearing. Bottom line was that there was nothing that was going to get in the way of me and this Jesus that Carman was talking about. I was the furthest away from the stage and the first one to make it to that altar, I accepted Christ right there in Kansas City in a Carmen Concert. At that very moment I felt different; the love of Christ rushed in my body and flooded my heart. I knew I wasn't the same and never would be again. The love of Jesus had flooded my body. The only way I could explain it was that I had never really felt love before, but now I felt like I was curled up in the lap of a loving daddy and that everything would be ok if I stayed right there.

Steve and his wife Susie became like parents to me mostly because David wasn't a good father and I really liked having a man in my life. I loved my mother very much, but it was like a blindfold was over her eyes. She just didn't have the ability to see the life she was in or she was just so worn down that she didn't care anymore.

Finding Jesus

Learning to Live Life

Though I had gone down and received salvation at that Carmen concert, I still tried to lead a double life. I was a junior in high school and people expected certain things from me. I was "that guy". You know, the one that is the life of the party. Looking back I pretty much was an idiot. I still drank on the weekends and smoked pot, but I did slow way down on the powders.

We had a new years eve lock-in for our youth group one year, and a Christian band called Rushing wind was playing. Something happened that night for the first time. During a song the lead singer stopped playing and walked over to me and whispered into my ear that God had called me to something great and that I was a leader. This was the first time in my life I ever heard anything like that, and I couldn't imagine myself doing anything great for God and as far as leading people, I was only good at leading people astray.

A few months later, I went with Matt to a local promise keepers meeting in Iola Kansas one night and had really been struggling with this double life and had considered just leaving it and going back. I would rather be a full time sinner than a part-time Christian. At the end of this, they had a prayer time. I walked down not to pray for myself, but to pray for my family. David had recently been arrested and held on manslaughter charges in Texas, and the whole thing was really bringing mom down. While I was kneeling down, I heard this thunderous voice speak over me. This man spoke with authority that I had never heard before, he shouted "Get up!" When I didn't, he commanded me to "Get up!" So, I stood, and then, he told me to raise my hands. I had never raised my hands in my life; I came from a church that sang three songs, had an offering, a short message and then we are out. Only crazy people raise their hands—you know, the holy rollers, the Bible thumpers, the Jesus freaks. I was compelled to raise my hands. Even though I did raise my hands, I was scared because I was thinking that if I didn't, this man would have my head! He prayed for me in what I thought was Spanish or something at the time. The prayer was so intense that I felt like falling down. I had never felt anything like this in my life. Matt later said he couldn't even put his hands on me during the prayer because of the power coming though me and out the other side of my body. After the prayer, the man took me to a private room and read my mail; he knew everything I had been doing, and it wasn't like some slide of the hand parlor trick; he knew specifics about my life. He introduced himself as Reverend Phillip Honeycutt. He asked if I went to church. I told him I did, but that I

Learning to Live Life

was sure interested in more of what I felt out there in that prayer.

The next day was Sunday, and Matt and I both skipped Colony Community Church and went to Honeycutt's church. And it was like nothing I had ever seen. It was electric—as soon as we walked through the doors, I got goose bumps. Then I heard praise and worship like I had never heard before. The churches name is Covenant of Faith Christian Center and it is a non-denominational Spirit filled Full Gospel church. People prayed in a funny language, danced, held their hands up, shouted things like amen and Hallelujah, then Honeycutt laid it down like I had never seen. This was a kind of preaching I didn't know. It touched me; it got inside of me. I realized immediately that that was where God wanted me. At the end of service that day, they had an altar call, and Honeycutt called me forward and prayed over me. He gave me a word from God. He said that God had called me to something great, and that I was a leader. I looked at him in wonder. I remember thinking how can these two people tell me the same thing. I had no radar for words of knowledge or the prophetic, and it was all blowing my mind.

Matt and I started attending Rev. Honeycutt's church, and I started learning so much about the supernatural side of being a Christian. I had a friend named Phillip Watson. Phillip and his mother where both Spirit filled believers and had been talking to me for sometime about the Pentecostal style beliefs. I was very curious about the baptism of the Holy Spirit and speaking in tongues, but was nervous about it at the same time. One Saturday I decided I wanted it, so in their living room, they laid hands on me and instructed me just start praying and receive. I prayed and prayed as they muttered, spit and babbled in their prayer language. Then, it happened; I opened my mouth, and the very first syllable of an unknown language came from my gut and rolled off my tongue and across my lips. That one syllable sent a shock wave through my body like electricity arcing from two posts, and I stopped. It shook me so bad that I decided I didn't want it. It had freaked me out because I was seeing with the natural eye instead of seeing with the supernatural eye. One syllable of one utterance, and it shook me that hard. Wow! The raw power of God is amazing!

The following Sunday, I walked up to the front of the church, and I told Rev. Honeycutt that I wanted the Holy Spirit. He laid hands on me and prayed. He let me know that all I had to do was ask, and I would receive it. The same thing happened as the members of the church stretched forth their arms and prayed in tongues. I could feel the moist hot breath of Honeycutt on my cheek as he would laugh, pray, shout and call down the Holy Spirit. It was as if a lighting bolt struck, it had hit me again; from the bottom of my gut, it bubbled up through my body, out of my throat, across my tongue, and over my lips; and then, like a flood, the unknown language, the language of angles poured from me.

I stood frozen in the Glory of God for what seemed like hours praying and praising in the spirit, pouring out in this new found spirit language with tears running down my face. Honeycutt then laid his massive hands on my forehead, and the spirit hit me hard again. My legs buckled underneath me and there was not a thing I could do but fall to the floor, where I continued to cry out to God in tongues. I couldn't do anything but lay there and think how wonderful God was.

This experience changed my life. I walked down the hallways of the school praying out loud, "Praise you Jesus , thank you Lord, I love you Jesus, Amen, Hallelujah, thank you Jesus." I found myself praying and I couldn't stop; it was like a light had been switched on in me and the darkness had to flee.

People looked at me in puzzled ways not sure

if I had lost my mind or not, but I didn't care what the world thought of me; I was in love with Jesus and I knew that I knew that he was in love with me too.

That was a really strange time for me because I had fallen in love with a girl for the first time in my life. Valerie was such a sweet girl, and I knew that we would spend the rest of our lives together. We where engaged to be married; the plan was that as soon as graduation came we would elope. Something strange happened to me: God spoke to me and told me to stop having sex with her. DO WHAT?! A young man like me, a senior in High School with a smoking hot girlfriend, and God was going to tell me I could'nt sleep with her?

So, for the first time in my life, I acted in obedience and told her. I remember the look on her face, she was so mad at me. I think she thought it was something about her. I tried to explain that I was listening to God, but she just didn't buy it. She ended up leaving me for some race car driving, air plane pilot. How could I compete with that?

Matt had gone on to college; he had decided to go to Ozark Christian College in Joplin, Missouri, so I decided that I was going to attend College as well. I had preached a couple of times, and I was ok at it. I

Learning to Live Life

had won a scholarship for my preaching at a Christian Camp that I attended that summer in Thayer, Kansas. So, I was off to another chapter of my life.

CHAPTER ELEVEN
CHRISTIAN COLLEGE

Christian College

The summer months leading up to my leaving for Christian college should have been filled with prayer and mediation, and instead, the stupid old devil got in my head, and had convinced me that I wasn't good enough, that I should have never thought that I would ever be able to be a man of God. I should just go ahead and party. This is what I did every single day that summer. I partied and slept with girls.

By the time it was time to head off to college, I was back to doing dope again. I went anyway and was so proud of myself because no one else in my family had ever gone to college. So, I packed my car up with clothes, drugs and porn to go off to Christian College to become a preacher. It was almost a stereotype for a televangelist from the 80's.

College at a Christian institution is a trip. They were not a spirit-filled school, but I never would have thought that me being spirit-filled would be an issue. Because I wasn't raised in the church ,I had escaped most of the religious stigmas that become intertwined into the doctrines and personal beliefs of people. But me being spirit filled was only the beginning of the issues for me.

The first week, the staff called everyone to an

outside area where they gave a nice little talk about something. I would guess holiness or strongholds something to that effect. All I know is that when they called for people to bring the items that they shouldn't have in there dorm rooms to the fire pit, I watched as people would throw in a CD or a book here and there. When the conviction of God hit me, I had to fill my trunk up and drive my car down where I emptied porn and music and drugs into the fire. The look on all these little sheltered faces was priceless. I might as well have driven a dump truck down. The Spirit of God let me know that I could not go into this journey half way. He wanted me Hot or Cold. Either get in or get out. It all burned, and with that, my body started to burn in withdraws.

For a week my body was wrecked with withdraws. I could swim in the puddles of sweet, and my body was completely aching from the flu-like symptoms from the muscle pain of my body jerking nonstop. I laid on that dorm bed as Matt, Mom and Dad Bear who where the dorm parents, and some others would come in and read scripture to me. It was a real Jesus moment as they loved me to health and nurtured me as my body and spirit both came into alignment. I came out just fine in the end, and after a week, the shakes went away and my apatite came back right in time for classes to start.

Christian College

I was really doing well at my first shot at being a real student. I had never really tried at being a student my whole life, so in return I was never a good student. Lack of effort and ADHD was not a great combo. At some point, the enemy started to whisper in my ear. He would say things like, "Derrick why are you here?" and "You will never be good enough!" Maybe you should do some dope so you can concentrate." The voices were constantly ringing in my head over and over. I can almost hear that condescending evil murmur now.

I started to think of drugs night and day, never using, just thinking. I didn't know what to do; I couldn't shake it. I was left with two choices: Do the drugs or ask for help. I decided to ask for help. I went to my dorm Dad first, and he then suggested that we go to the school dean, who happened to be out of town. So, we met with the assistant dean. He suggested that I go to a state rehab facility for a month and "learn" how to "deal" with my problems. Wow, I left that day and for thirty days, I sat through teacher after teacher telling me that I would be and addict for the rest of my life.

After a month I sprung myself out of the treatment center and came back to college. First thing the next morning, I was summoned to the Deans office.

He sat on his side of the awkwardly large redwood desk and peered over at me. This is one of the most damaging, wounding moments in my life, as he said to me, "We don't want your kind here."

As I took the long walk from his office to my little dorm room, I cried. I had twenty-four hours to vacate the college; I didn't know what to do or where to go. That night I tossed and turned all through the night and somewhere between falling asleep and waking up, I had decided that it was Gods fault for what had happened to me, and when that man looked down his long nose of judgment, it was God looking down at me. How could a God that loved me so much do such a thing to me? I would never go back; I was through with Christianity and Church.

Christian College

When God and the Church Don't Want You

"We don't want your kind here" rang through my head for years. When the Christian College kicked me out, it rocked me to the core in a bad way. I was devastated. My life was a train wreck. I felt like a zombie walking around with no purpose. I had planned on serving God for the rest of my life, and me being a young immature and naive person, I thought that in order to serve God, I needed mans approval with a piece of paper that said I had earned a position to be able to serve God on the level that I wanted.

I went into a deep depression, a spiral that I was not sure even had a bottom. I was so lost and so desperate, but for what I had no idea. I moved back home to Colony Kansas, the only place I knew to go. I rented a house there and tried to forget about the God that I had wanted to serve.

I of course used everything that had happened and everything that was said as a reason to use drugs and drink again. I took a job in the city and drove 2 hours every day one way to work building houses. My boss ended up being a great weed connection, and I partied it up for several months. It was the hard kind of partying. Even though I kept a job, I'm not sure if I ever slept. The door never stopped; people coming and people going. Then one night, I had my door kicked in by the State Troopers,

From Death to Destiny

Sheriffs department and the city marshal. It was so strange since I watched the whole thing from the house across the street. I sat in my friend Romel's living room and watched as they ransacked my house. Come to find out they had received information that I was a member of the mafia and had moved back from Kansas City.

After the raid I packed up what I needed out of the house and moved back to Joplin. I moved in with a buddy that I had met at church camp years before. Jeremy was an awesome free loving hippie, and he absolutely loved to smoke pot. We smoked pot from the time we woke up until the time we went to bed—wake and bakes, snacks, lunch, and dinner. I smoked so much pot in those nine months that I should still be foggy.

It really didn't take long before I started pushing the partying to the limit. At this point, I was doing a couple of grams of Meth a day, using cocaine on occasion, dropping acid and eating mushrooms as much as I could. I was so deeply depressed that I was finishing every night with a pint of Everclear. I would drink until I would black out. When I blacked out, I didn't have to feel the pain anymore.

It was in this dark place that death came

knocking again. He presented opportunities to take me deeper in to the mouth of the beast. I was really good at fighting; it was something that I was a natural at. You can train people to fight, but good fighters where born to fight, and I was a born fighter. To make it better I was 225 pounds and 6'4" so I was a little intimidating as well. I was hired by some local drug dealers to start collecting money from those that wouldn't pay their debts.

It was an exciting life for me; I would walk up and kick in doors—walk in with a baseball bat in one hand and a pistol in the other. I was a get-results type of guy. If you didn't pay up, I would take everything you owned in your house and leave you bleeding with your kids watching in horror.

After kicking in hundreds of doors and breaking hundreds of faces, it wasn't hard to move up the ranks of the drug business. Because I had so much success in collections, I was asked to step into underground fighting. This was back before Youtube and street fights on reality television. Most of the fights where organized by crooked cops or the mob and often times both had their hands in the pot. Everyone called me the "Knockout King" on the streets. People would try me but would never last. My signature move was the right hook to the temple that would cause the other person to fall into a huddled mass and go into a seizure. They would be shaking like a leaf with their eyes rolled in the back of their head and one arm up in the air shaking. I was fighting twice a week, and I fought this way for eight months. It was taking a toll on my body, so after a while, I went back to just selling drugs and collecting money.

My paranoia was spinning out of control, and my roommate suggested that I get a job to take some heat off me. So, I started working at this little telemarketing company setting up appointments for rainbow vacuum cleaner salesmen. I met Callie at this company, and I started hanging out with her here and there. The first time I went to her house, I met a crazy couple of twins. Lee and Tim—super skinny, black and crazy. These guys like to do three things: Drink, fight, and party. They always had a forty of Miller High Life in their hands. Lee and I had a lot in common; he had been a preacher at one point in his life and had fallen away from it. Lee had let the "church" push him away from his calling. So, in looking back today, I can see that he too was drinking his pain away. Lee also had a gang affiliation with the CRIPS just like I had. From that point on, Lee and I were pretty much inseparable. As a matter of fact, the only reason I got into the relationship with Callie was because of Lee and I's friendship. Callie was cra-

When God and the Church Don't Want You

zy. As a matter-of-fact, people called her crazy Callie, not that I was any better. She would take on grown men and win, sometimes I was afraid to go to sleep at night fearing that I would get a ball bat in the rib cage for something I had said the night before.

Lee and I started a click, and it wasn't long before we pretty much ran things on the drug seen. If you wanted it, we had it, if you needed it, we could get it. Bigger dealers would pay us to go in on products or to get money that was owed to them. At that point, we were the big dealers. I would take trips back and forth from big cities with product. We would drive around town with pockets full of cash and drugs. I was known for carrying a sawed off shotgun. I had the world, including all the women I wanted waiting in line.

At this time in my life, my favorite thing to do was to kick in the door to a drug dealers house. I would take everything: all the guns, all the drugs, and what were they going to do about it? Call the cops—no way. 99% of people were all talk, and they knew that I was the guy that would say I was going to shoot you and I was the guy that would follow through with it.

We had a rival drug dealer send a sergeant

to our house one day. I beat him up and chained him up to the toilet in the bathroom for a couple of days. Before we sent him home, I carved my initials into his chest. This is the type of attitude that was necessary to make the kind of moves that I wanted to make. You come against me and my people and I will carve you up, and you will never forget me.

Some one attempted to off a rival drug dealer, and it landed him in the hospital on life support. I thought it would be a great idea to rob his house while he was dying. I took a guy named Mark with me to do the job. We kicked in the back door and started loading up anything of value—stereos, TVs, cd's, guns, and then I hit the mother load. I found close to a half of Kilo of Cocaine under the bed and two ounces of peanut-butter dope in the freezer. It's called peanut-butter because its not washed of the impurities to make it pretty white. People also call it shooter dope because the high is better to those that shoot it up. While I was in the freezer, I also took all the steaks just for good measure.

I loaded all this stuff up and took it to my apartment. The whole time I was still living with Jeremy at some old apartments. I turned that place out. We had nothing but a huge party. Our entire floor turned into a party floor. It wasn't uncommon to come in and people be passed out in the elevator naked. The landlord was a short, mousy, irritating guy who was strung out on coke. The funny thing was that he was getting his coke through me and didn't know it because the maintenance guy was his connection, and I was the maintenance guy's connection. So, the Landlord had a level of paranoia, and what was about to go down triggered it big time.

The guy that helped me rob the house got so spun out because I gave him a speedball. A speedball is a shot of cocaine and meth in one shot. Well, Mark decided to rob my apartment while I was gone. When I showed up ,Jeremy my free loving hipie friend was heart broken that I would let this happen to him. The landlord freaked out because he was high and the cops were coming. I was evicted on the spot and was banned from ever coming back. I really damaged the relationship with Jeremy, and things were just never the same.

I moved into Callie's house and had lived there for a couple of weeks when lee showed up in the middle of the night and said we're going to jail tonight. Turned out that someone had disrespected him, so we went back and turned the heat up. We went over about 10 deep and I blazed the place up with a shot gun then a pistol. By the time we pulled out of the housing complex, we had a string of cops already in pursuit. I drove a 1985 Cuttless with a sun roof, and I smashed the gas pedal and there we went. My first bonafide high speed chase through Jasper County, Missouri. City, County and state officers were all in on the chase. We ran till we couldn't run anymore, and after a brief stand off on the side of the road, I received a couple of blast to the face with a mag lite until I went to the ground. That's when the kicks to the ribs started, and what was I going to do about it when I had 30 some officers with guns pointed right at me. The next stop was county jail.

Lee, Tim, their older brother Mike, and yours truly took up permanent residence in the county jail. My boys went on to population, but I went straight to solitary confinement. I just couldn't stop pushing the limits. I was coming down from being high and in a rage from being beat up by the cops, so when an officer got locked in sally port with me, I took advantage of the opportunity and took him to the mats. I beat him like they beat me. Law enforcement didn't like that much. I received another healthy beat down from several officers with a side of pepper spray and couple of days strapped in the chair. So, as others went to general population, I went straight to solitary confinement.

When God and the Church Don't Want You

I spent 3 weeks in my boxer shorts with no toilet, no sink, and no bed. I was able to leave my cell once a day for 30 minutes to walk in a slightly larger cell, use the restroom and make a phone call. If I didn't get a bathroom trip in, I would have to use the hole in the floor and have no toilet paper. I had no choice. I couldn't get out because my bond was $250,000, so it was time to get used to it. After a couple of weeks in there, for some reason, I found myself singing praise and worship songs and even the occasional hymn. I found my sanity in God. "He came from heaven to earth to show the way" I would sing as loud as I could. "AMEN, PRAISE THE LORD", I would shout as loud as I could. I would rant and rave about Jesus and the Bible. The Lord showed up in the belly of a wale for me and pulled me through. After a few weeks, they put me in general population.

The next seven months were a breeze as they made a mistake and put me in the same pod that Lee was in. It was like camp. Just as fast as I let God back in I forced him right out. I didn't go to prison after all because Lee took the wrap on the whole thing telling the judge that he was the shooter. Since he had never been in trouble, they gave him probation. They gave me timed served on the chase, but the cop beating never came up. It was most likely because they had to get rid of all the footage because they beat me right after.

A few weeks after being released from jail, Callie came in and gave me the surprise of my life. "I'm pregnant", she informed me, and I was stunned. There was no way I could be a father; I didn't want to be a father. I wasn't father material. Callie and I didn't get along; we where always fighting and not just arguments. She had what was called explosive personality disorder. She would punch me in the face and the next minute want to kiss me. I was young, stupid, strung out, and in a corner. I chose the coward's way out, and I ran. I left her freshly pregnant, and I had zero intentions on ever going back. I know now that it was a mistake and the wrong thing to do, and I have since apologized to Callie for what I did. I think it was so easy because it is what was done to me; my father ran out on my mother and never came home—this was what fathers do.

CHAPTER THIRTEEN
A NEW LOW

A New Low

My cousin Nick lived in Emporia, Kansas and he was able to get me an apartment through his landlord. I cashed in some savings bonds that my grandma and grandpa had giving me every year. It was enough for me to pay first and last months rent and the deposit. I had planned on keeping to myself, working and trying to keep my nose clean, but you can change your playground and playmates, but if you don't change yourself, your always going to go right back to the same old thing. Within my first few days there, a neighbor came be bopping over with some cocaine. He called himself Jacks and had a tattoo of a ball and jacks going around his arm. He said the strangest thing to me. He asked me if my name was Ducky? I didn't know how to answer. I just looked at him. He said a cop had stopped him and asked him if he knew me. It was only three days and the cops were already looking for me? Good grief. Well, I partied with jacks and he and I hit it off. I was off and running in the same direction as always, straight to hell.

I was so high; it was like I was diving into mountains of cocaine and snorting my way out. Every dime I made went right up my nose. My landlord smoked weed, so I was paying her that way. We started selling cocaine to support my three-hundred dollar-a-day cocaine habit.

We hustled a hookup straight from the Mexican mob. I will never forget the day that I walked into Jose's club house. In the club house there was brand new leather furniture, about ten naked women laying around or dancing for strung out guys, music bumping some base heavy Spanish rap, big screen TVs, and guys with guns everywhere. After sitting there for over an hour not sure what to do, a stereotypical Vato walked out of a back room and motioned me in with no expression on his face at all. I stepped in with Jose, his door slamming shut behind me and locked. His door guy searched me for weapons but I wasn't holding anything but cash. Then Jose pulled out a drawer that had at least a kilo of cocaine in it. It was customary for the Hispanic and the islanders to have you take a taste of the product in front of them. He asked to take some, and I had learned that you don't want to just put anything in your body; you could get a hot shot.

A hot shot could kill someone on the spot, or it could kill you slowly. That's when you put some chemical into the drug. People would put Ajax in dope sometimes to make people sick or kill them. So, when he asked me to do the drugs, I simply asked him to do some first. Jose was glad to oblige my request and he laid out a thick line of the white powder then snorted it all in one long graze off the mirror

A New Low

with a rolled up Hundred dollar bill. With a shake of his head and a single tear rolling down his cheek he gave me the go-ahead nod. I was more than willing to do a line like I just seen him do. I was ready to get high, but he stopped me and pulled out a spoon and syringe. I was quick to let him know that I didn't get down like that, but he immediately looked at his door guy and gave me a look. You can tell a lot about a man by the look they give you, and I could tell you that he gave me the "either you do it this way or you will get a bullet in the back of your head" look. I knew that either I slammed that cola or I was going to end up in a ditch somewhere. With about a 25 second hesitation, I took the long reach for the syringe.

Now I was not a shooter but plenty of my clients where shooters through the years, and I have even hit plenty of veins for junkies that couldn't hit it for themselves because of being to junked. I had said that I would never shoot up, but I had never been that great at keeping commitments. I pulled up fifty cc's of water and put it on a pile of cocaine in the spoon. I used the plunger to stir the cocaine and water together. I pulled a cigarette filter out and bit of a small piece and rolled it in my fingers and dropped it in the spoon. I watched the cotton absorb the liquid cocaine. The needle then went into the filter were I pulled the plunger and watched the syringe fill with the thick substance. I took the syringe and held it in my hand taking one last look at Jose and his door man knowing that one way or another I was dying. One way was instant and the other way would kill me slowly. I chose number two and sunk the needle into my vein pulled back blood then I slowly pushed the plunger as the liquid entered my body. My head started to echo and the sound a train was racing through my head as I fell to the floor. Jose started laughing at me and his voice was triplicating. I knew in the first moments that I was in trouble and that I would never go back to snorting drugs.

My arms became pin cushions always bruised and scared up; It is a fast spiral after you take that road. I became sick so very sick, and death was knocking again. The next 6 months was a goulash of events that dragged me even closer to the fire. Strong armed robberies, drug heists, more fights than I could count, women and a stint in Mexico.

Mexico was great, but Lorado was a very dangers border town. It was and still is in the top three most dangerous cities in the world. Police were on the corners with machine guns, and the government ran prostitution and drugs. Boys town is a complete part of the city that is nothing but bars and hookers; the streets are lined with little rooms just big enough

A New Low

for a twin size mattress and a box of condoms. The bars were sleazy, smoked filled rooms typically with a stage in the middle where girls would dance or perform sexual acts with animals. The government would run a bus from the American side over to Boy's Town all night long; in the bus were a bunch of American truck drivers spending their families' checks on cheap tequila and dirty hookers. I could see opportunity in the midst of a border town. After a bad run in with two dirty border town cops, a drag queen prostitute and a pimp that was higher than I was, we decided that this trip was coming to a end. But, I knew that I would return to Mexico.

Our car was so saturated with the pungent odor of random drugs that the dogs hit our car at customs automatically. They would not leave us alone because the dogs were going ape. I literally think the dogs where smelling the cocaine coming out of our pores. US customs made us empty our entire car out and they searched everything, and whoops, Cole forgot a syringe in one of his bags. Then the hours of interrogations and strip searches from immigration and customs officers started.

Hours later we rolled out of the customs station and didn't stop until San Antonio. The only thing I knew about San Antonio was that that's where Ozzy

Osborn urinated on the Alamo. We hadn't been there an hour when I got in a fight standing in front of the motel. The old Indian man at the counter called the police then it started all over again with the searches. The San Antonio police where convinced that we had the mother load hidden someplace. For hours, I sat cuffed behind my back in South Texas heat in a plexiglass enclosed backseat of a cop car. I watched as they tore out sheet rock in our room and brought dog after dog in. They also brought in one of those construction lights so they could drop the tank to our car. It was ridiculous and all for nothing. We didn't bring any drugs with us. The reason I know this is because I wasn't high; if I would have had drugs, I would have been high—follow the logic. Eventually the police sergeant gave up and slowly the cops pulled out leaving us with a mess and one ticked off Indian clerk. When I went in the office that smelled like a curry chamber the next morning, the man wouldn't even speak to me. I guess we had it coming.

About 5 hours into the 18 hour drive, I started to think about the fact that I had burned out my stay in Emporia. The Cops were looking for me, I had robbed too many drug dealers, and I was to strung out to keep a posse together. I also started to comb through the happenings of the last 7 months and came to a conclusion that Jacks was a cop. It all went back to the very first conversation that we had when he asked me if my name was Ducky. He told me that a cop had stopped him, and it finally hit me that he was the cop. He had been working me to find out all my drug connections across the United States. I was backed into a corner with no protection from either side of the law. I only had two places to go—back to Joplin or to the country to live with my mother. Joplin it was!

I needed a ride from Emporia to Joplin, so I called my friend Matt, the one that I was roommates with in college. I told Matt that I had a bed waiting for me at the drug treatment center in Joplin, and I needed him to come pick me up. Matt being the champ that he was, drove five hours to get me. He then took me five hours back to J town with one extra piece. Jacks decided at the last minute that he wanted to come with me. Holy cow! This man is a cop, and he is really pushing it.

We got to Joplin and I immediately gave Matt some line about needing to get something before I checked into rehab, and I rolled out on him. Jack wasted no time, wanting me to hook him up with some meth connections in Joplin. I kept putting him off. My first priority was a place to stay. What better place than at Callie's. I knew that she was about to have the baby, but I had no clue where she lived. After a few hours ,I found someone that knew her new address. I walked the ten blocks to her house and as I came up the sidewalk. I could hear her say, "Oh my God! It's Derrick." I walked in to find her, her friend Alisha and some tall black guy named William. In a matter of seconds by glancing around the room, I could identify that this guy was living there and more importantly, he was sleeping with Callie. I did what I did best—I punched him in the face about three times and threw him past Jacks and through the door. William never came back. It was a good choice for him.

I laid in the bed that night thinking about the fact that I would be a father in a matter of days. A thousand things were racing through my head, and I decided that I was going to give this thing a shot. For the first time in a very long time, I really was going to try to go straight. I dropped Jacks off at the flying J truck stop and told him, "Sorry, but I was going clean cold turkey and couldn't help him any more." That was the last I heard from Jacks. I found out recently that he had told everyone that I had overdosed, and they left me in a ditch someplace in Missouri. He did this because I think that he knew that I was on to him and didn't want anyone of my friends specifically Cole trying to find me.

A New Low

Now living with a woman that I didn't love expecting a baby any day, I went to work for a company packaging parts for a barbeque grill. I really intended on making a go of it. I hadn't been in the place for more than four days before someone asked me if I wanted to get high. Come on, cant I do anything right? I had already made the mistake, so I went off to the races slamming dope.

The next week Savannah was born. She was so beautiful and I was truly a proud papa, but I was not ready at all for the stresses of being responsible for another human life. All I had ever done was let people down, hurt people and destroy lives, and I was really concerned that I was going to destroy Savannahs life.

Because Callie and I didn't get along, ever, I used it as a reason to stay out all night, sometimes not even coming home for days or weeks. I had started using Meth again instead of cocaine because the high was longer, but meth gives you a paranoia that is unexplainable. I started spending a majority of time with some guys named Reddog and Troy. We all had the common interest of getting high and not letting anything in this world stop us from that task.

I was very young, and these guys where old

school. They met each other in San Quentin prison. Reddog was probably the craziest guy out of anyone I ever ran with. He was a tattoo artist from Santiago, California and was an old school gangster to the very core. He lived and breathed crime. One time he told me that the reason he tried to kill a guy was because he wanted to go to San Quentin. I said why would you want that man? He replied, because the Q is good for the resume. These guys were not your everyday gang bangers; these guys where hardened criminals, and they took me under their wings to show me a whole other level of hell.

Reddog would rip you off to your face and make you like it. At the time, I thought it was funny. I became scandalous just from being around them. I would smile in your face as I was stabbing you in your back; it was just the attitude that I had, and it was the attitude that it took to survive in the dope world.

I was getting sicker, ever so close to death as the drugs where eating away at my body and my mind. I was hiding my addiction from Callie by shooting up in the bathroom, and if I stayed all night at the house, I would lie in bed and pretend to be asleep. This by the way is a talent. The relationship with us just wasn't there; I couldn't stand her and she couldn't stand me. Finally, I just left.

A New Low

If I had never gone all the way in the world before now, it was time. I spent two years learning the art of manufacturing methamphetamine. This was convenient because now I could just make my own drugs. I was now one of the biggest producers and suppliers in the region. I was doing over three grams of drugs a day. Pumping the dope into my arms and pushing my body to the limits is what I would do. I would stay up twenty and thirty days at a time getting so junked out that I would sit on top of the house with night vision and a AK-47 shooting into the trees because I could swear the feds where coming. Cooking dope had become just as addictive as doing the drugs. That's all I needed was another addiction.

I was asked by some white supremacist for some guns, and in a moment, I realized that I was missing a whole network of money. I tracked down some old connections in Texas and worked my way into a deal transporting guns, drugs and occasionally women across the border from Lorado, Mexico to San Antonio Texas. I had plenty of men and the cartels were always looking for people that weren't afraid of going to jail. My guys weren't afraid because I kept them too high to say no. The job was simple; we would drive across the border where I had leased a small room in a cheap motel apartment building, and my guys would post up in my room until the cars were delivered across the street. The keys were left with the desk clerk, and we would grab the keys and my guys would leave at the same time to cross the boarder. When they arrived at the destination, I would meet them and settle up on the mule fees. We typically wouldn't know what was in the cars, and I liked it that way because at times I would have guys working for me that may have jacked a car if they knew that they had eight kilos of cocaine in the door panels of the car. If they would have jacked the car it would have been the same thing as me jacking the car. We would usually make those moves twice a month. I made 5,000 a car that made it to the destination. It didn't matter if it was filled with cocaine, heroin, AK-47 assault rifles, pistols or a couple of women doped up in the trunk. So, on a good month when no cars got hit by customs or boarder patrol, I would make $50 grand after paying my guys. I was walking fat with thirty large a month.

More money didn't mean anything to me because I could party away 50 g's in cocaine in a week. Throwing parties, paying security, and feeding drugs to the women; it all goes quick. You're always running more just to keep up with the party. I never had enough money; I never had enough drugs; I never had enough death.

A New Low

All this money; all these drugs; all this death. Why wasn't I happy? Why did I just keep consuming and consuming? It was getting out of control; I could feel something wasn't right. So much blood and so many broken people—death and destruction.

The end was coming one way or another. Death was breathing his hot breath on my neck. Back in Joplin one night, my buddy Reddog told me of a new cook that he thought I may be able to get to work in our lab, so in the middle of the night a guy named Aj and myself drove to the small Kansas town of Galena. We walked into a small grungy redneck cookhouse. The dope was so thick; it was eating the paint off the walls. This place was so white trash, junkie. They had two babies running around that looked like they where pulled out of the garbage dumps in a third world country. They had diapers that where exploding with waist running down their legs and dried snot all over their face. I remember them rolling around on the floor chewing on cigarette butts, lying around. Sorry to say, all that was actually a good sign for me. It meant that number one, they where high all the time, number two it was good enough to keep them high, and number three because they were so junked out, it would be no problem for me to get them to work for me. I waited on the couch for the cook to come out, and when he did, he brought about a pound of fresh-off-the-pan meth out in a punch bowl. He looked at us and said, "Help yourselves." I reached in my jacket pocket and pulled out my rig bag as any class act junkie would. Reddog went first pulling up a thick 50 and blasted it; he immediately ran to the door coughing (coughing is the effect that good dope will have on you; mostly it takes your breath away). I was super competitive about everything, so I pulled up a thick 90. There was more than a gram of dope in that one shot of uncut meth.

    The shot of dope was so thick that the bubble of air wouldn't even come to the top. I had to swing it like a baseball bat to get the bubble to rise through the syrupy super glue like liquid so I could register the shot. I thumped my left arm in the crease until my vein popped up almost like it was hungry for the needle. I slid the needle through the permanent hole in my arm, and I released the plunger, and it went to work. A quarter of the way through the shot, everything turned green, and then my head started to spin. At the half way point, I passed out because it was too much. Aj thought he would do me a favor and push it the rest of the way in; this was not good for me. I woke up with my head spinning and my heart racing. My blood pressure was so high that I could see my heart beating in my eyes. I told the guys to get me out

A New Low

of that place. They drove me back to Joplin and the only thing I could remember about the trip was everyone and everything was green. Once we hit town, Aj was driving the wrong way down a one-way street, and I had warrants, so I gathered myself and said "let me out". I walked a block to a hooker's house that I tricked out on occasion.

She and her husband were going to meet a John, so I laid on the couch and tried to stay calm and focus on getting my head together. My heart started to skip beats, and I panicked. I went into a paranoid, anxiety, soaked, rage. I tore down ever picture, threw the TV through the window, and stumbled to the yard. Death was kicking in my door. I crawled up the neighbor's steps screaming for an ambulance. He cracked the door and said he didn't have a phone. As a lay in the yard, my vision narrowed until I could see nothing.

My eyes opened occasionally as the car would throw me from side to side as it hit potholes, and I could see the stop lights out of the rear window of the car. Lucky for me, the prostitute Chris and her husband Wally had pity on me, and instead of leaving me in a ditch to die like most drug addicts would, they took me to the hospital. The car slid up into the Saint Johns hospital emergency room, and Wally tossed my body out in front of the doors as Chris yelled for emergency workers. They then sped off so no one would ask them any questions.

I was so high that that my heart was not functioning correctly causing me to go into cardiac arrest. They shot me up first with morphine, but the nurse administered too much, and it stopped my heart completely. After several minutes of resuscitation, they brought me back to life. I remember as I came in and out of consciousness, the nurses and doctors were trying to find veins for IVs. They were talking about how junked out I was and how disgusting all my track marks were.

I spent two weeks in the hospital recovering from the over dose and heart attack. When I first woke up in the room, I couldn't believe I was still alive. After the first day when I really was able to come to, I couldn't believe what I looked like. At the time of the heart attack/ over dose, I had been awake for thirty-three days straight and had not eaten the majority of those days. I was basically alive on the will to cause more trouble and Gatorade. My face was sunken in where you could see my bones. I could hardly stand because I had no strength in my muscles. I was so dirty that the nurses and doctors had left my pants on me. I had this horrible stimey smell from all the

A New Low

chemicals seeping out of my pours, and my pants were like stiff cardboard because I hadn't showered or changed my clothes in twenty-five days. I was a filthy junky and the nurses didn't even want to come in the room; I was so disgusting. I couldn't stand my self.

I got out of bed, yanked the IVs and probes off my body, and stumbled to the bathroom were I just stared at this strange person in the mirror. "Who am I", I wondered. I tried to take my pants off, but they literally were becoming one with my skin. I had to peel them off, and skin was coming off with them. Strangely enough, in my back pocket was a spoon and a syringe. Choking on my own stench, I tied the bed sheet around my neck and the other end to the shower nozzle and dropped to the ground. I was searching for the embrace of death, but as death scurried towards me, the shower head broke, and I fell to the floor. The nurse was banging on the bathroom door.

For the next week, I just laid in the hospital bed in the dark with no visitors. I had instructed the hospital not to let anyone know were I was. Death may have lost the round, but round two was taking its toll on me. Depression was an unforgiving foe. After eight days in bed and not one word spoken to anyone, my first visitor showed up. Reddogg peered at me through the door with his beady eyes. As scandalous as Reddogg was, I think that he truly loved me. He came barring gifts. He emptied a sack out on me of playing cards, porn magazines, Cheetos and a Reece's Peanut Butter Cup. He then asked me, "Do you want me to bring you some dope?" Surprisingly enough, I said, "No." Because I was so deep in depression I just wanted to stay there; I didn't want to live. The next day, two unwanted visitors darkened my door—Callie and my mother. First of all, I didn't need Callie's nonsense, and I definitely didn't want to see my mother or for her to see me like this. I turned into a nasty, vial, snake. I lit my mom up like the fourth of July, calling her every name in the book; death was talking now—all the withdraws and hurt were spewing out of me, and it had locked eyes on my mother. I told her what a horrible mother she was and how I hated her and never wanted to see her again.

I crawled out of my hospital bed and backed them both out of my room screaming and screeching at the top of my lungs about how much of disappoint she was, and how it was fitting that she raised a bastard of disappoint like me. I threw my hands up in the air with my butt hanging out the back of my gown, and asked her if her little junky has made her proud today. All the nurses and doctors had stopped

A New Low

in the hall and were just staring at me. With a demonic howl, I said "WHAT ARE YOU STARING AT!" Then, I spit at her and slammed the door. What she doesn't know is that I went back to my bed and cried for hours. I regret saying those things to my mother; I love her very much and always have, but like they say, "You take things out on those that are closest to you."

After much time of just laying in the bed, I decided to walk out in the middle of the night. I had some girls pick me up at the end of the hospital, they drove me to the dope house. At three in the morning, I'm was in a old smoke filled crack house, sitting in an old leather recliner in nothing but a hospital gown; I still had my IV in and little probes all over my body. I was nodding out from a shot of Heroin. Heroin is what I knew would take the depression away because I wouldn't think of anything while I was nodding.

From Death to Destiny

CHAPTER FOURTEEN
GO BIG OR GO HOME

Go Big or God Home

The next thirty days was maybe as close to Hell as I could get. I was dropped from our boarder business because the guys across the boarder thought I was too much of a risk. I was lucky that they didn't kill me. I had to come up. I had obligations I needed to take care of, like putting a needle in my arm and keeping my minions high, so they would do what they're told.

A war broke out against my group and some others. It started with me trying to get up on some soft. Soft is cocaine before they rock it up into crack. Crack has a portion of baking soda in it. That's what causes the cocaine to take a hard rock like form, and that's why they call it hard. Well, in the hood, if your not careful, you will end up with all baking soda or even worse a bag full of wax or something dumb like that. The Mexicans in town were laying low; most of them were in jail or deported because of a sting that went down. Because of that, I had to go to the east side to get my soft. When Caleb came back to the spot, he didn't have soft; he had a kilo of hard. He brought me a kilo of the wrong drug. Let me show you why this was a problem. I was paying 10,000 for a kilo from the Mexicans, but in the hood, I had to pay 18,000. You can turn a kilo of uncut soft for around 50,000 on the street, but we would put a little cut on it and make around 65,000. If you get a kilo of hard, it means that it already been cut with baking soda, and you cant tell how much baking soda is in it. From experience, they would cut it by half then rock it up. So, basically what was happening is they were taking 32,000 out of my pocket. And that was not going to happen to me ever. Someone had to die.

My driver pulled the car over, and I yanked Caleb out and put my pistol in his mouth. He was screaming not to do it as cars sped up to get by us. I pictured my trigger finger caressing the cold metal strip just enough to set a chain of events that would end with the hollow point 38 mm bullet blowing a chunk out of the back of Caleb's skull right on the side of the road in broad daylight. Lee started screaming out "D...D.......DDDDDDDD, NOT HERE NOT NOW"! I then took my pistol and beat Caleb with it until he was in a pile of flesh on the ground. On the way to the crib, Caleb agreed to take the drugs back and get the money back. I'm not real sure if he really thought that it was going to work, but I knew for sure that it would not and that things where going to get real deep real quick. When Caleb left, the last thing I told him was either you come back with the money or you come back with the drugs, but if you don't come back with one of them then he might as well just kill himself.

Go Big or God Home

Caleb went back to the east side where he went into the house and stole the money back. I'm not sure to this day if he took all the drugs back or not. The east-side crew knew that Caleb had taken the money, and they soon were out to get us. Several of us were going out in the country to one of our cook spots one night when two SUV's ran us off the road, and what came afterward was something out of the Wild West.

Jason jumped out first shooting double handed. Jason was a horrible shot and emptied his clips quick as he took a hit in the shoulder. I crawled in the back seat and got through to the trunk to get the shotgun. Glass was shattering everywhere. Jason was screaming with blood gushing, and Trevor and I where hunkered down in the car waiting for the gunfire to let up. Then, it did. I jumped out and unloaded the shotgun blowing out every window in the suburban behind me, then, I got hit from behind. My head was throbbing, and I could feel the blood running down my neck. As I rolled over, I squeezed off three rounds from my pistol striking one of the men in the hip. I thought I was going to die, and as I looked back to Jason and Trever, I could see another man coming towards our car, so I fired one shot randomly towards him the best I could, striking him in the left side of his face. I was out of ammunition and not sure where we where on ammunition, but they burned out. I laid in that ditch and told Jason and Trevor that I was dying; death had finally won. Trevor started laughing hysterically at me and said your not dying. As I rolled, over I saw the bloody tire tool. I didn't get shot—I got hit. We took off to the hospital—Jason and I went to different ones to get fixed up. Two more gun fights happened that month as far as I know nobody died.

I was so paranoid that I left my car somewhere and couldn't remember where it was. My feet where blistered and swollen from walking in a paranoid frenzy for two days, so I stole a cab and drove it to the block that Callie lived on. I would only go there when it was convenient for me—when I needed to sleep for a day or hide from the police. In spite of her abusive nature, I was also extremely abusive both emotionally and mentally. She wouldn't let me in that night, so in traditional "me" fashion I just kicked the door in. she was screaming and yelling threatening to call the cops, so I tore the phone out of the wall. Then went to lie down. I can honestly say that I'm not sure what happened, but the next thing that I remember was me straddling her on the couch with my hands wrapped around her neck. She was dark purple with tears running from her eyes and blood from her nose. As soon as I realized what was going on, I threw myself backwards off her, and I began to cry and beg for her forgiveness. I was not one to hit a women; I never had. I seen my mother go through it, and I just would not do it. It was death creeping in on me. She never spoke of it again.

I was slipping farther down the slippery slope toward the fire of hell. Everyday seemed to me a new low for me. Chris one of the hookers that I would trick, the same one that her and her husband dropped me at the hospital, she came to me one day. Chris was pregnant and wanted to get rid of the baby. She wanted to take a massive shot of dope, get high, and abort the baby. I stared at her in the eyes contemplating what she was saying. The look on my face was emotionless as I tossed the idea around. Chris then pulled out two hundred bones and I immediately agreed. I hooked her up with a master blaster shot of dope and since she couldn't hit her own vein, I hit it for her. It was about two hours later she was on the bathroom floor screaming and holding her lower stomach as her blood stained pants laid in the bathtub. I murdered a baby, I murdered an innocent life. What was wrong with me.

Things where too hot with the cops and with rival crews, so we started lab hopping. When we were cooking meth, we started using a portable lab. When cooking the Red and Black method it was easy to be portable because one didn't have to gas anything. We would rent kitchens from people. I paid them by the job. If I was doing a big cook, I may throw them a zip (ounce). If I was just burning a small batch like an ounce, I would throw them a gram or two. A skilled junky could take two grams get high and still make two-hundred bucks, but mostly they just wanted to get high. My meth was in high demand because everything else was trash, or they where getting ice which was junk too. Most times in the labs, there is what are called bag whores that hang around and act like they are concerned about you and want to help and usually offer sexual favors to the cooks and dealers. I usually ran these kind of people off because I knew they just wanted free dope and typically they where going to rob you some how.

This night for some reason I let this strange lady stay. I never had seen her before and never seen her again. As I was banning off a batch, she said to me, "You know, this is going to kill me" I responded and said "what?" She repeated, "This dope; it's going to kill me—I cant stop". I sat that pan down right in the middle of the cook and looked her right in the eyes and said, "Do you believe in God?" She said, "Yes." I then said, "Do you believe the bible?" She replied, "Yes I do", and I then said, "Do you think that when Jesus healed the blind that they were still blind?" She said, "No." Then the spirit hit me, and I went with it. "God wants more for you than you being in this dope house in the middle of the night. He can take this from you right now; you don't have to live like this anymore. You can have complete freedom." I then said, "But who am I to preach at you." She sat there and looked at me crazy, and I went back to cooking.

There was no doubt to me that some sort of shift was happening within me but I didn't know how to, or what to do, so I just kept doing what I knew best and that was doing wrong.

Checking Out

Six more months of brutality on my body and mind came and went. I started to cry out for death. Death would be so much easier than living. Death would be a welcomed friend. I was getting even crazier than I ever had been. I was using five grams of dope a day and now my crew was completely gone. Scared of being shot or busted by the cops, I was lost; I couldn't even cook dope anymore. I had gone from a guy that had things and ran things to a guy that had nothing. I was a low life junky now. Not even a functioning junky. I was sleeping in allies because I was too spun to make it to my car. My car was my home. It was snowing and I would just do more dope to make the pain of the cold go away. With no money, I was back to dropping people. I would just target the drug addicts and take the product from them. I had cracked so many faces that my knuckles were completely swellen and broken open. I was back to not showering and I had gotten and infection under my skin in my arm where I would shoot up. I had stopped into the emergency room faking some sickness so I could steel some rigs from the ER room, and I called one of my girlfriends Angie.

Angie took me to a place way out in the country to score some dope. She went into the house and about an hour later she came out; I'm sure she was having sex for the drugs but I didn't care all I cared about was the fact that she came out with a eight-ball of dope. I put a gram and a half in a spoon then stuck my rig in my bottle of water and pulled up twenty-five cents; I squirted that twenty-five, and I was left with a past something almost like cookie dough that wasn't going to go in a syringe. So I dove in the water again, another twenty-five. I put it in the spoon and it was massively thick but I was able to draw it up. This shot was bigger and thicker than the one that killed me earlier that year. I knew I was getting ready to die. I then slowly and meticulously worked the bubble to the point of the needle, I knew that I was getting ready to step out of this realm and into the realm of death, and it was exciting me in some strange sick way. I massaged my arm as I watched Angie sink her needle deep into her arm and plunge the drug into the blood running through her veins. She immediately started to tweak, making sexual suggestive motions to me and at the same time, she couldn't stop looking around from the instant paranoid rush. I rubbed my vein trying to get it to pop but it just wouldn't, I was too dehydrated and my veins were all blown out from to much abuse. I tried between my fingers and between my toes and then straight into my wrist but I just couldn't get the blood to register. I was now overly irritated and frustrated. I was ravagingly hungry for this and nothing was going to stop me. "Angie do the heart stopper" that's what we called the jugular vein. She looked at me in shock and said, "No D there is no way." I yelled at her to do calling her profane names.

She crawled over and straddled me; I then nervously cocked my head over and she started to tap the side of my neck, massaging my vein until it began to show itself. She then sunk the needle into my neck, and I took a deep breath and began to fly. I could feel the air under me as I lifted off the ground and everything became white. In a second, I took a nose dive and went into convulsions. Blood was dripping from my nose and the last thing I remember was the lights going out. Angie started to scream as she fell out the passenger door from on top of me, and the drug dealers came storming out of their trailer slapping her in the face demanding that she get me out of there. She took off down the country roads calling an ambulance during the drive. The rescue workers met us on a back road and moved me from the car to the ambulance. By the time I arrived at the hospital, I was barely alive. Out of instinct, when I would come to just a little bit, I would rip the IVs and hoses out. The doctors instructed security to come in and strap my arms down. At some point my heart finally gave out and death's persistence had finally gotten the victory he had worked so long to get.

Jesus Encounter

As I passed through my flesh, I found myself outside my body looking down at that complete stranger that had been running my life for years. My arms were strapped straight out to the sides of a cold lifeless human carcass. I can't explain the feeling except that I was being tugged by a negative energy. I would've guessed that it was death and his minions dragging me to the pits of hell that I had earned for my sorry excuse of a life. I had thought that I wanted to die, but I had unexpectedly found myself not wanting my life to end now that it was gone. I then noticed a presence in the corner, and in an instance, I had this knowing that it was Jesus.

I didn't see him in a physical form; it was more of a spiritual encounter. I cried out to him and said please Lord take this from me, take this addiction and let me live, but if you don't take this addiction, I will still kill myself; and if you spare me, I will serve you for the rest of my life. Like a flip of a vacuum, I found myself back in my room awake and alert as the doctors and nurses were around me with paddles and needles. God had grace and mercy on my life; God had spared me. Praise God that I never used drugs another day in my life after that encounter. God had healed these blind eyes; he set this captive free, he took it away just as I asked.

From Death to Destiny

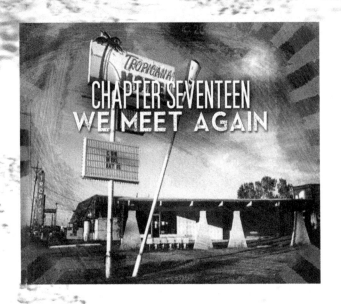

CHAPTER SEVENTEEN
WE MEET AGAIN

We Meet Again

God always kept his end of the bargain he made with me, but I haven't always been the greatest at keeping my end.

I had never lived a straight life, and I had no clue how to proceed. I just walked blind and hoped that I did the right thing. I knew that most people who I had ever seen that were living a straight life where married so I figured that was what I should do. I couldn't even remember what my daughters face looked like, but I thought it was a good idea to marry Callie. She wasn't home, so I left a note on the door that said that if she wanted to get married that I would do it. Needless to say, she wanted to get married, so that week we slipped down to Miami Oklahoma and got married in a little white wedding chapel with two of her friends as the witness's. Married now, I went to work and tried to live the best I could.

Although I didn't do drugs and run the streets like I once had, I did still drink quite a bit with my brother Lee and some new friends. Life had changed but death was still pursing just in a different vehicle.

One day my mother called me and said that my father wanted to see me, I replied with "tell him to come on". She said no. Your biological father wants to see you. I was more than a little shocked about what I was hearing. I hadn't seen him since I was two. I really had no desire to see him unless it was me hammering his face with my fist. I reluctantly agreed to meet this sperm donor.

For a week, I sat and thought about what I was going to say or if I was just going to smack the teeth out of his mouth. What do you say after twenty-five years? Mom, My father Doug and I met at a little hotel lounge called the Tropicana, the place has long been destroyed now. He pulled up in this little S-10 style pickup truck and got out. I sat in our SUV and couldn't stop thinking about how short he was. I stepped out shook his hand and we went in to have a drink. I really didn't say much; I just listened to my mother and him chat back and forth. All the things that I thought I would have said and all the things I had planned to do to him if I ever saw him went straight out the window, and I just let it go. He called me that night to see if he could come meet me again and to apologize for running out on me and not being in my life. I opened my mouth with the opportunity to say all the things I always wanted to say, and this is what came out: "You know Doug, life is filled with a lot of should of, could of, would of's. We can't do anything about the past, we can only change the future." I had just come to a place where I didn't think it was going to do anyone any good to set up camp

We Meet Again

in the past. There was nothing that he, my mother, or I were going to be able to do about it. Doug and I became close over a couple of years until he married and then cheated on my mother again. After that he took off and married a 2nd or 3rd cousin of his. It never surprises me how strange my family could get. I'm guessing based on my experience with the demonic that it was a classic case of generational curses. I have bound and broken this evil off of my life. Thank God I have'nt felt the urge to leave my wife for a cousin.

From Death to Destiny

CHAPTER EIGHTEEN
THIS PLACE AGAIN

This Place Again

Even though I had a miraculous healing from my morbid addiction to drugs, I was still not living my life to a standard that I would call Godly by any stretch of the imagination. I was kind of going by the good ol' boy policy. If I was just a good ol' boy and didn't mess around on my wife, didn't screw anyone over, didn't hurt anyone that didn't have it coming, then I would be ok with Jesus and he would be ok with me.

I still had an appetite for excitement, so I would throw a lot of big parties and still drinking a lot, but only socially. I still had one little problem that was very apparent. I still had a temper and loved to fight. The whole key to my fighting now was I would wait for someone to look at me funny or someone I was with. I would press them until they threw the first punch and at that point, it made them all mine.

One fall night, I took my biological father, who was now engaged to remarry my mother after twenty-four years, to a local bar called the Southside Tavern. It was a dive of a biker bar. My friend Terry Hanson's band called Total Access was playing that night. I was fifteen shots of tequila, two pitchers of bud light, and three backdrafts into a good buzz when a guy pushed my wife and she stumbled and fell. Well I really didn't care that she stumbled and fell, but what I did care about was that this was my chance to get my wreck on. I Stood up and abrasively put two palms in his chest bumping him back about two feet; the bar got quite and started to divide—you could quickly see who was with who. The man had about seven or eight good size guys stand up with him and made some smart comment about taking me out. In my drunken state, I took the wooden bar stool beside me and crushed it on the floor screaming, "I don't see one person in the entire bar that can take me." The fight then took off—fists flying, bottles breaking, pool sticks shattering and my dad fighting at my back. Doug was no stranger to fighting as this was more than likely the gene pool that my talent came from. One of his friends told me a story of them in an all African American bar. They were locked into a poker game when a fight broke out and he pulled his knife and carved his way out. This was the very scenario happening at that moment—fighting our way out of certain defeat. Bodies laid everywhere and blood soaked my clothes when the so familiar red and blue lights reflected and bounced around through the alcohol branded mirrors and advertisements. I quickly moved off to the dance floor where the band started playing again. The cops came in from every door looking for me. After blending in for several minutes, someone finally pointed me out, and I was politely asked by the police to follow them. They wouldn't try to apprehend me because they knew who I was. I told the officer that I would think about coming out as I grabbed a beer off of a table next to the dance floor.

I eventually followed them out to find thirteen officers waiting to apprehend me. I then backed myself into a corner and challenged them to come get me. My mother was screaming at me to stop as the police lined up. Fighting a cop was no different than fighting anyone else to me. Then the duty sergeant stepped up and kindly asked me to just go home. He said "Derrick we don't want to do this again. Can you just leave and go home"? I respected that, so we called it a night.

This was kind of my routine. During that season, I went to college studied hard worked as a mortgage broker and I would spend my weekends fighting in the bars. I just couldn't get it quite right.

Bags Packed

Callie and I just didn't get along. I was not a good husband to her and she was not a good wife to me. There was excessive baggage from the past. Our marriage was out of control. Some think that it is funny, but the reality was that I was an abused husband. She had broken my nose two or three times, stabbed me, and hit me with a car a couple of times. She was out of control. We would leave each other every other week; it was no life to live. But something had been really off for some time, and I just couldn't put my finger on it, so I moved out into a little motel room to get my head right. The next day she reviled what it was. She had been sleeping with two of my friends. She was having an affair; I couldn't believe it. What I couldn't believe was that she would think that she could get away with it, and that the two guys would think that I wouldn't make them pay. I still had half of my mentality dipping into death, and he was creeping back in and loving every minute of it.

For some reason, I thought it would be a good idea to get back at Calli for sleeping with my friends by sleeping with her friend. So the same week that we split, I called her friend Jennifer who I had seen give me "the look" several times in the past and asked if I could come over. I was trashed drunk and lucky for me her apartment was just a few blocks from the Red Lion (what a great name for a bar, the

Red Lion). Stumbling drunk, I walked into her apartment and within ten minutes, we were in her room having sex.

I broke her heart because she thought that I was actually interested in her, but for me it was merely retaliation. I later found out that one night of retaliation breathed life into a little girl. She was a pretty little girl. After much thought about it later, I had decided not to pursue a relationship because she has been raised with a father who she thinks is her real dad. I just felt that I would destroy her life by wrecking what she thought was her family.

Two weeks later at a bar one of the guys that slept with my wife showed up, and I was with a bunch of friends drunk beyond drunk. I nailed him on the dance floor, bloodying his nose and some lumps on his head before he knew what was up. It wasn't the kind of beating that I felt he had coming. See death was whispering in my ear to kill him. Or better yet, tie his dead body to her so she could stare at the bloody mess that she caused. The bouncers separated the fight and kicked us both out. When they released me, he had already been gone for fifteen minutes, but he was hiding in his truck. Death wasn't done yet.

I jumped up on the hood of his truck and

punched the windshield until there was a hole big enough to pull him through. I pulled him out and went to work. My fist was the meat hammer and his face was the steak. Then a friend of Lee's, some Mexican guy, pulled a pistol and asked me if I wanted to shoot him. So I grabbed the gun stuck it in his mouth and pulled the trigger. People scattered as blood splattered and the sirens rang through the air. Death got what he wanted. The boyfriend was dead and I was going to death row. Except I never pulled the trigger. I played the whole thing out in my mind, and at the last minute, I dropped the pistol and dropped him. I never shot him; I just thought about it. Even though I didn't shoot him he was still hospitalized, and had to have facial surgery. He will remember that day for ever.

That night twenty-five police officers raided my little motel room with swat uniforms and dogs. Another night in Jail—I was used to it.

Through this whirlwind a friend recommended that I try this internet dating thing, and although I fought it, I did eventually give in. The first day I started, I talked to a girl from West Virginia named Marissa. It was great because she told me all the sweet nice things I wanted to hear. We ended up marring each other just after only seeing one eachother physically seven times. Marrissa was a down home southern type of girl, very quite and reserved. She was a good girl having never done a thing in her life; we were complete opposites. This was going to be a trip and not in a good way.

Bags Packed

From Death to Destiny

CHAPTER TWENTY
GOD CATCHES ME

God Catches Me

I was sitting on the steps of my apartment one winter night, and I was thinking. Thinking of all kinds of things as I would take a drag off my camel wide cigarette. I was watching the snow dance across the parking lot in the glow of the streetlight. Something attracted my eyes up to the sky, and it was strange how the stars seemed to wink at me. I couldn't help but to see the beauty of God resting upon me in that moment. I then said aloud to know one but me and God. When is tomorrow going to be too late? I knew the truth; I knew that I wasn't living right, and I would always think that I would get right next week or just one more party or one more fight. When is tomorrow going to be too late? I told God that night as I smoked that cigarette that I was done, and I was coming home.

I had an awakening that night, a real awareness of the world that surrounded me and a understanding that certain things must change. Lee showed up the next afternoon with a case of beer. The look on his face was comical as he sat on my couch staring at me as the movie played. He couldn't believe that I told him that not only did I not want to drink but in fact, I didn't want to ever drink again. Come on D he would say. Just have one with me for old time sake. I responded, Lee its been less than twenty-four hours; this is not for old times sake.

Days went by and Lee would come over with a sixer, and I would turn it down. Days turned into weeks and I cleaned out my refrigerator that was full of beer and liquor. I think Lee squeezed a tear out the day I poured it all down the sink.

I worked as a loan officer at a local mortgage company and one of the other officers was also a youth pastor at a little Baptist church. He was the only one I knew anymore that was a Christian, so that's where I went. The look in his eyes when we walked in was priceless. He had asked me to come to church a thousand times and nine hundred and ninety nine times, and I didn't show up. Marrisa and I sat in the back row of that little Baptist church, and I listened to every single word that rolled off that preacher's mouth. I made it a habit; we started coming every Sunday, then Sunday turned into Sunday and Wednesday, and then Sunday and Wednesday turned into Sunday, Wednesday and small groups. I couldn't get enough of God.

One day I woke up and my filthy mouth was just gone. My mouth was so foul that it would make a sailor blush. But God just took it away. I didn't try; it just happened.

One Sunday during church, I found my mind

God Catches Me

slipping back to Honeycutt's church. While everyone in the Baptist church was sitting on there hands singing old hymns, I was thinking of running the isles screaming praises at the top of my lungs, jumping up and down, rolling on the floor laughing. The Holy Spirit was calling me back to the Power of God.

From Death to Destiny

City of Refuge

I had a friend named Jack and he had been attending a little church in Baxter Springs. Baxter was a small town that neighbored Joplin over on the Kansas Side. He was saying all kinds of great things about the pastor of this church, and some how I came up in conversation, and the pastor wanted to meet with me. Pastor Dan not only pastored the church, but he also had a ministry called City of Refuge. COR would go from town to town setting up small concerts to draw the youth and unsaved. Almost immediately I started helping his traveling ministry. I had a more modern style, so I could relate better to the younger generations.

The church that Dan pastored was called New Beginnings, and it was a Spirit-filled church. The name was even fitting for me, so I made the jump from the Baptist church to Dan's church. This didn't sit right with Marrisa—she was born and raised Baptist and had never heard anyone speak in tongues.

Jam for the Lamb

Life for the most part was good. I had graduated college, was several years into being a broker and now heavily involved in church. One thing that really was holding me back was the fact that although I had love for Marissa and cared about her, I was not in love with her and never had been. But I tried; we kept moving forward, but it was like two friends sharing a house.

God really started using me more and more. Speakers would come through and speak into my life about some sort of greatness, and I still didn't see it, but I pressed in. I started online and correspondence courses for ministry to push myself further in with the Lord. Looking back you could really see God grooming me for something more. It wasn't long before Dan asked me to take position in the church as an associate Pastor. This was a huge milestone for me because years before I said I would never step foot back in a church. Dan and I had thought about doing a big event for several months; we had a great amount of success with our parking lot and park events. We thought about it for a while and finally came up the idea of doing a Christian Woodstock.

While we worked on this big event, we also moved the church from Baxter to Joplin. We planted a completely new work. Even though Dan was the senior pastor I pretty much did all of the ministry work and church planting. It was a great experience to go through. We started out by renting a small room off the greyhound bus station. We ministered to a lot of homeless people, and that is where I really developed a heart for the less fortunate.

In May, we produced our first major concert. It was off the chain, crazy-cool. It was a funny thing that we held a rock concert at a Precious Moments park in Carthage Mo. I think we had about five thousand people come and go over the weekend. We had lots of testimonies by some great friends of mine at that time, people like Bill MacLemore the author of Meth What's Your Destination, Denise Ledbetter author of Methed Up, and Pastor Honeycutt from one of my home churches. We had something like twenty bands over the three days with each night ending with a major label act—Day of Fire, Krystal Myers and Overflow to name a few. They were all relatively famous at that time.

When the last night was coming to an end, I stepped out after Day of Fire rocked the stage, and a guy walked out behind me and played Amazing Grace softly on an acoustic guitar. I opened my mouth and the Holy Spirit started to pour out. I didn't know that I had it in me. As I walked back and forth on that big stage testifying about what God had done in my life, people began to move forward; my spirit was connecting with theirs, and God was using me. I shouted "Jesus, Jesus, Jesus! Say it with me! Jesus, Jesus, Jesus! If you want what I have found…if you want what God has for you, don't walk. Run, run right now and knock down this fence. I want to pray for you right now."

Then it happened. The Spirit of God fell and hundreds of people ran forward to get prayer. People fell out on the grass, people cried, people shouted, people were healed, people where delivered, people where saved, and people were moved.

I went backstage that night and cried my eyes out. God had used me in that way, and I didn't feel worthy of it at all. I told him that night that if that was what he wanted from me, then I would do my very best to not let him down.

From Death to Destiny

CHAPTER TWENTY THREE
PREACHING MACHINE

Preaching Machine

"The Spirit of the Lord is on me, because he has anointed me to preach good news to the poor. He has sent me to proclaim freedom for the prisoners and recovery of sight for the blind, to release the oppressed, to proclaim the year of the Lord's favor."

Luke 4:18, 19

After the Godstock event, I had several awakenings in my life; the main one being simply that my call to minister and preach never went away despite me walking away from Christ for so long.

I did a swan dive deep into the word of God placing him before everything. I would witness about my testimony to everyone I would meet. I started to speak at churches and conferences and started to work in the gifts of the Spirit. I remember the first time God used me to heal a women. It was amazing that God would use a wretch like me to do his work. I had no clue about who I really was, who God had made me.

I may not have been ready, but I was willing to be used and willing to go anywhere and do anything. With the success that Dan and I had with Godstock, I thought it would be a good Idea to start a production company. The idea was to produce big concerts and develop new Christian talent. We did a bunch of small park concerts, parking lot rallies and several mid-level events around the four states with a few thousand people that would attend.

One day Dan called me and asked what I thought about becoming a Baptist church. I didn't understand the reasoning behind it. I was still green when it came to ministry. I just really knew enough to get myself into trouble. He explained that the Baptist denomination was willing to fund our church if we would make the jump to become a church in the denomination with them. I didn't feel right, but I didn't know what it was. Dan and I drove to Springfield, Missouri for a week of church planting classes and at the end, they licensed both of us. At first nothing changed, but as time went by things got really strange. The Baptist leaders in our region started coming to services now and then, and one day they insisted that we denounce the gifts of the spirit and stop operating in them. I may have not been in ministry very long, but I immediately got a check in my spirit about this.

Coming one day from work, I found out that Marrisa was pregnant. I was excited about it because, I thought it maybe something that would bring us together, and maybe I would fall in love with her. After a couple of weeks, we went ahead and started telling people and toying around with baby names and all the typical things that people do when they find out they are expecting a baby. She was so ecstatic, and I was excited for her. About a month in, she started getting the extra room ready, and we bought one of those baby name books and started a list of boy names and girl names. I had never seen her with this much joy.

Early on a Saturday morning I could hear the screams from the bathroom as I pushed the door open Marrisa was on the floor clutching her stomach and blood was everywhere; my mind flashed back to the baby that I helped abort with the drugs, and I was in shock. After a few minutes, I was able to get her to the car and I rushed her to the ER. We lost the baby that day, and I believe I lost the last bit of Marrisa that day too. We were both heart broken, but there is a connection for a woman that I don't think men have. She was really wounded.

From Death to Destiny

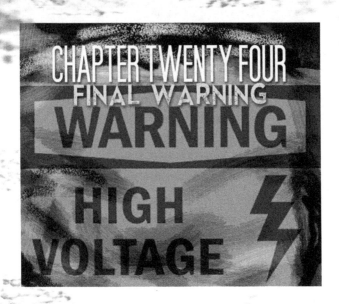

CHAPTER TWENTY FOUR
FINAL WARNING

Final Warning

All my life I loved to sing even though I had not been really confident about it. It was something that had not been nurtured by anyone in my life. I had started singing in church and it seemed to take off for me. I started a good classic rock style Christian band called Final Warning. We played a lot of different venues and churches. One of my favorite places to play was a recovery group called Saturday Night Live. The group was part of Central Christian Center, which is probably the biggest church in Joplin. When we first started playing, it was a group of about twenty-five people. We were asked to play on Thanksgiving for a big celebration that a bunch of groups were coming together for. It was a lot of fun, and I just really liked the direction of the church.

Some of the local ministries decided to do a revival at memorial hall, and Dan had asked our band to do the worship for it; so we agreed. This group of musicians were some of the best musicians in the area, and we were really good. Dan gave us a list of songs he wanted us to do for the revival because they would go with the theme. What seemed like a blessing turned out bad.

We worked hard for weeks to prepare for this revival—night and day rehearsals. I was freakishly serious about the band being tight. We were excited, but not for the reasons we should have been. It wasn't about the ability to share Jesus with people; it was about playing in front of people and the approval of men.

We showed up the night the revival was to begin at memorial hall and sat up on the massive stage, sound checked in, and was ready to rock! Then one of the pastors came up and told us that they had someone else doing the worship because we were too "rock and roll" for what they wanted. Instant rage ran through my body as my blood boiled. They wanted us to stay after and play a concert so that's what we did and we rocked it out. For three days, we would show up with the intentions of rocking the stage and nothing for sharing Jesus. We were so arrogant, as we would sit back stage and not even come out and listen to the speakers. Our bass player was even drinking at the time. My mind was not on the ministry, it was about my flesh.

I did something at that point was very immature and not honoring to Dan as my spiritual covering. I was so ticked about not being the worship band and aggravated all around about the Baptist situation that I just left. I dropped off my key in the church and walked out the door the last night of the revival.

Final Warning

I didn't understand that God will have you in places sometimes to teach you whether you are in agreement with him or not. I definitely didn't understand that; I shouldn't have left unless God told me.

The same week I started attending Central Christian Center, and within a week, I put together a new band to do worship for the recovery group. They took me in at Central like part of the family. They where huge. Central had four thousand members— that was way bigger than anything I had ever been to.

I became great friends with Big Kenny. Kenny had been an outlaw biker with a %1 group. We had lived very similar lives and even knew many of the same people. The strangest thing was that we had never crossed paths. Kenny and I grew very close, and he became like a brother to me.

The guitar player in our band, Chris, was a member at Central and Chris had become like a best friend as well. We were pretty much inseparable. We played music together, went to concerts together, worshiped together and we would even get up at 4:30 am and go work out together at the gym. He was such a shredding guitar player and had some of the same history that I did. Finally, two people that understood me. Chris and Kenny!

Over the next few months, the recovery group grew to one-hundred and thirty people. I was doing ministry for the church and heavily involved in the community. Everything was going great for ministry, but things at home where not. Marrisa and I still had no change. We would go to church and smile then go home and live separate lives.

Marrisa and I bought a little house, and when we moved in I jammed a wooden wall ornament into my eye and scratched my cornea. It was amazingly painful, and I couldn't stand it, so she drove me to the ER where they treated me. Typically, this kind of injury although painful, heals quickly. The doctors and nurses where surprised when I turned down the pain medication. The nurse said that she never had anyone turn down pain meds. She then handed me a bottle of eye drops called Novocaine. She said just put it in your eye when it's hurting. So, for the next two days I used this drop every twenty minutes unknowingly burning away the nerve endings in my eye.

The very second that I ran out of the eye drops I knew something was terribly wrong. The pain was worse than at the beginning. I was screaming and writhing on the ground because the pain was so out of control. I was rushed back to the hospital to find out that I was loosing eye site.

Final Warning

I was referred to an attorney and soon I had a lawsuit for several million dollars against the hospital for malpractice. My attorney was strict about what I could do and couldn't; he forbade me to go back to work until the suite was over. At the time I really didn't have a problem with that. It gave me time to do ministry. I could only do things for a couple hours at a time before the headaches would put me down, but since I was on my own time I made it work. I was doing full time ministry.

Something about being a minister that is important is that your spouse becomes just as part of what your doing as you are, and Marrisa did not like the life of a minister. She didn't like the always on the go lifestyle. She loved the Lord and wanted to love me, but we where just too different I guess. I came home early one night from a ministry event, and I heard the door quickly close to the bedroom, as I walked to the back I noticed the light on my laptop was on so I sat down and raised the screen. She had been on the computer and when the keys rattled the doors, she shut the top and ran. Marrisa had left the chat screen up and it reveled not just one guy, but two that she had been having an affair with. She had not only been talking to them online, but it reveled times they had met and engaged in sexual acts together. I was enraged! I calmly thought it through; I knew things like this could destroy a ministry. I thought to myself, "What do I do?" I first copied all the conversations to CD, so I had proof of her infidelity. Then I sat and chewed on it and chewed on what was happening. The whole time she was in the bedroom, and I'm sure she was sweating bullets about what was going on with me in the living room. The entire time I could feel this scratching at my spirit, like a knotting of my stomach and heart. Then a darkness slid over me as I could feel every ounce of joy that I had exit my body. Then like a possessed, man I stood and walked to the bedroom and kicked the door in. I screamed at Marrisa to get up and pack her shit. I got right in her face and screamed at her calling her a cheating whore and how I hoped she would die. She cried and kept trying to hold on to me as I would shove her back. She cried out that she was sorry and that she loved me. Loved me?! Is this what love looked like. I know that she was just looking for what I couldn't give her, but in the heat of the moment all of that escaped me.

I didn't end up kicking her out that night; I just slept on the couch. I actually didn't sleep at all; I cried. I couldn't wrap my mind around why this always happened to me. About five in the morning, the enemy came creeping into my ear, and I remember like it was today as I'm writing. This is what he said: "Derrick, you will never be anything, you will never be happy, you will never have anything, nobody will ever love you, and you will never be able to love. The only thing that you are any good at is doing evil. Lets go get high. Lets do it! You know you want to; it will make all of this go away. Just stick a needle in your arm Derrick. It's the only thing that you really love its the only thing that makes you complete."

I sat up on the edge of the couch, and the thought of shooting dope again oddly made me sick and excited at the same time. This is probably only a feeling that someone that has done dope can relate to. I didn't want it, but I wanted it. Death was pulling me; the enemy had a foot hold on me.

Still in my clothes from the night before and no sleep, I got into my car and took off. I was going to go get some dope. I said aloud, "I just want to hold it in my hand". I thought that if I just held it, something would make me feel better. That was a lie from the pits of hell. I couldn't drive anywhere without seeing a house that I had done drugs in, cooked dope in, sold drugs out of, or had a gun fight in. It just wasn't possible because I had done so much dirt. In the past when I was paranoid, I sometimes would stash drugs around town in bushes and gutters in case I needed it. Every block I encountered something. And every lie that death spoke God would remind me of the pain that came with it. Every time that the enemy would say do it, God would show me what happened when I did. God was good to me that day as he always was. He didn't stop me from doing the drugs; he just encouraged me to see how far I had come.

Instead of jumping of the cliff back into the world that day, I went to the church and sought wise counsel. Doug and I prayed that we would fall in love, and that I could let this go and forgive Marrisa.

Doug was a wise man and had become such a great mentor in my life. He was always right. What was funny was that he would never tell anyone what to do. He would just bumper you into seeing the answer already in you, and then you would think it was your idea. He was great. Such a great man of God.

Final Warning

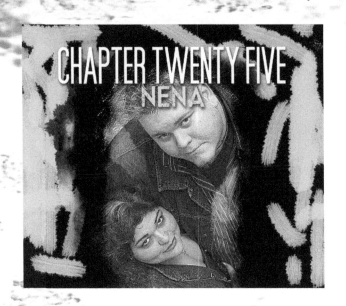

Nena

Daryl Had a ministry that was kind of overseen by Central. It was a Christian sober living program house. At the time, the program only involved staying clean, going to church and going to the recovery meeting. Although some would say it was to loose, I would see the effectiveness of it time and time again. The church had asked me to help Daryl with the ministry, so Marrisa and I ended up opening up the woman's house. This was good for us because since I couldn't work at the time, money was very short. We moved into a big house, and soon we had fifteen women staying with us. I grew to love helping people. To see them come in broken and see them gain confidence and self-worth again was a unbelievable blessing. I knew that I would house people, for the rest of my life. It was something that spoke to my spirit.

Unfortunately things with Marrisa were not getting any better. I would literally sleep on the porch sometimes just because I didn't want to be in the room with her. I couldn't get past the fact she had given her body away to other men. So one day I just couldn't stay any longer, and I left.

I went and stayed with a buddy who had a men's recovery house. Then it happened; Marrisa lost her mind. She couldn't deal with the fact that I had left. She gathered up every possession that I had, every piece of clothing, every picture of my daughter Savannah, all the pictures of my past life, all the things my mom had given me that belonged to my grandparents, and burned them in a pile in the backyard of the woman's house. It was all over. She left that week and went back to West Virginia, and I have not seen her again.

This caused some drama in ministry; I stepped down from leadership. Of course people hated on me. I found out sometime later that Marrisa had told people that I had kicked her in the stomach so she would lose the baby. I just felt dry.

I pretty much walked away from doing public ministry at that time. What I mean is once you are called your always called. I had a woman who reached out on our band website who was really needing help, so a friend and I went over to her house. Melanie was very lost and to be honest her intentions were to try to get with me. I was venerable at the time because of Marrisa, and was just not quite right in the spirit. But I had told God that I never wanted to be with anyone again unless he put us together.

The first night there, I found out that she lived with another women and her daughter, and

Nena

she was the Nanny. Later that night the owner of the house came home and me being the outgoing person that I was, I yelled through the house at her a couple of times. She eventually came into her room and met me, and wow, Nena was a KNOCK out. Hispanic love. I was mesmerized by her stunning beauty and personality. We had a couple of conversations that week over the phone that lasted hours and then went on our first date. I remember it like it was yesterday how I couldn't keep my eyes off of her; she made my heart leap. I had never ever felt this before; it was amazing. I felt like I was constantly blushing. I prayed after that date, "God if this is the one you have brought me then we have to be equally yoked. God I can't go through the pain again. "

Sunday I worked security because the parking lot guy was gone. I volunteered because I would be able to call her. I walked the parking lot talking about everything, then I asked her what the name of her church was. She said Community of Christ, and I stopped in my tracks and my heart sank. I knew that Community of Christ was a Mormon church. Even though I was called to love all people I knew that we would not be equally yoked and that was the commitment I had made to God. I immediately told her that this would probably be a deal breaker explaining to her that it was important that who ever I was with be equal in our understanding of God. She explained that she hadn't ever believed in the book of Mormon, and it was just where her family went. From that day on she attened my church with me.

Within what seemed like days, we knew that God had brought us together. We loved each other so much, and it was the first time I had EVER loved a women like this. It was like God formed her and made her just for me.

One of my greatest memories of this time was when I met her parents. Her dad owned a successful music store in town ,and I had known him and her uncle for years. I actually bought my first acoustic guitar from them all the way back in 1997 when I was in Christian College. I shopped at the shop at least once a week and never knew that Ben had a daughter. Man I fell in love with her family too. Ben and Emily were just like parents to me. One day Ben actually gave me a hug and told me that I was the only man that Nena had ever brought home that he had liked, and he told me he loved me. Life was good.

Although we wanted to do the right things in the right way, we were unable to get married right away because she was going through a divorce from a short violent marriage. The guy was dragging his feet and changing dates all the time all because of me. So Nena and I did the wrong thing and moved in together before we where married. It was a horrible mistake on our parts. What little ministry I had left was burned to the ground and the enemy loved every bit of it.

CHAPTER TWENTY SIX
LOOSING IT ALL

Nena and I were so deeply in love, but it didn't help that something was missing in my life. I was so used to having church family, and because of my choice of living in sin, I felt that I couldn't go back to church until that changed. So I dove deeper into music to fill the void of ministry. I started a recording studio, managed bands and produced concerts. The studio was sick complete with sound engineers, photographers and graphic designers. We quickly picked up bands and artists and started having a ton of fun.

Things took off and companies and artists where bringing us to cities to listen to showcases and putting us up in the nicest hotels and driving us around in the nicest cars; things where really going good. To make things even more awesome, we found out that Nena was pregnant. This was an awesome surprise, and even though Nena and I had both planned on not having any more children, we were both surprisingly excited to share in this together.

With a whole lot of discussion with a group of people we decided to go ahead with another big Christian festival. Right away, I should have stayed away from producing anything Christian when I was living in sin, but we jumped in anyway. The plan was to throw the biggest music festival that the area has ever seen.

Things came together, and it was looking like this would be the event that everyone would be talking about. We had sponsor agents, security teams, stage crews, lighting specialists, carnival and food vendors, and not to mention, all the awesome bands. I was so excited and so was everyone else. 100,000 posters, post cards and fliers where printed, TV adds where ready to role on local and cable, radio adds where off the chain. How could this go wrong?

About four weeks before the event, I found out that my sponsor agents had never really got any sponsors. Are you kidding me? Everything that we did we based on sponsor money. When we would meet twice a week, my two agents didn't want to come empty handed so they made it up; they never had any sponsors. Wow. The only money that we had come in were from the vendors who paid a fee to set up and all that money was long gone on operating and advertising cost. With four weeks to go, we decided to make a push for it, and just get the money from the ticket sales. It would be close but our team was certain we would make it.

With two weeks left to go, I had a visit to our office. A local self-proclaimed prophet and a couple others came into my office proclaiming that God had told them that I should cancel the event. I hadn't heard God say that, but in honesty I was not really trying to hear God at that time. He flexed his Godly authority around my office spouting about how many thousands here and thousands there he had preached to, and I just didn't think that a true prophet would come in my office and brag. So, I politely told the group that I appreciated what they had to say, but I was going to let my yes be yes and my no be no, and I said I would do this concert, and I was going to follow through with my commitment.

Two days later I ran into an executive from one of the TV stations, and he asked me why we canceled the event. Do what!?!?! You can imagine my surprise to hear this little piece of information. I quickly drove back to my office and called every media sponsor. They had received the same answer. According to them, someone from my staff called and said we where canceling the event. This is not good, what now. We were done and there was nothing we could do about it. With out the media outlets, we would not sell the amount of tickets we needed.

We tried to do another event shortly after to raise the money to pay all the debt, and it just got worse. We went completely belly up when a newspaper reporter started making claims that I had never intended on doing a festival, and that I was just taking the vendor money and blowing it. What followed was something that I never thought I would go through. The storm of a lifetime was descending on me and my family, and it was driven by death and the taste that he had for me.

Within a week, the attorney general had put a restraining order on my company; every person I knew turned their back on me. The newspaper started running daily front page articles about me and how much of a monster I was. The TV reporters would park in my drive way or up the street waiting to see somebody. Nena was even assaulted by one, and the nightmare was just getting started.

With in two weeks, I was subpoenaed by the attorney general with a class action lawsuit, all fueled by this guys claims that I had set out to scan everyone. My attorney suggested that I not speak to the media even though it seemed like it made the situation worse because nobody ever heard my side.

Next were the death threats. People began calling, driving by and screaming. Bottles were being thrown, windows were being broke out of my house and cars, and there were gun shots. It had turned into a circus, and I was the main attraction. It was so bad that I had to move my family into a little hotel room.

The depression moved in like a fog rolling in off the ocean. It rolled up over me like a sleeping bag and the enemy reached down and zipped me up. Nena was pregnant and on bed rest with twins, and I couldn't get a Job anyplace because of the publicity. We borrowed what we could from my family and the few friends I had left, but the quick sand was taking us deeper and deeper. The courts were now going beyond public embarrassment and now trying to imprison me. Things where not looking good for me.

Driving through town (Nena was driving because I didn't have a license), and we where side swiped by a minivan. Nena was thrown into the steering wheel and she took the brunt of the force to her stomach. The ambulance came tearing through, and my wife was laying on the side of the road curled in a ball screaming in pain. The world was spinning around me as they all but threw her in the back and rushed off to the hospital.

I was in such a place with people that I didn't even have someone to call for a ride. Nobody would come pick me up. So I crawled through the passenger side of the truck and drove it smoking and spraying fluids everywhere on the way to the hospital.

I got to the ER and they wouldn't let me in the room to see her because we weren't married. I sat in the waiting room, pulling my hair out crying because they wouldn't let me in. Finally the door cracked, and they call my name. I rushed back to her room to find doctors and nurses frantically probing at her with ultrasound wands, trying to find the babies heart beats. Nena reached out and grabbed my hand, and we held each other so tight waiting and watching for any kind of answer.

Late in the night, they had finally found one faint heart beat. We had lost one of the twins. Heartbreak on top of everything else; how much more could we handle? How much more would be shoveled on top of me.

The pain that we were enduring mentally was indescribable. Spiritually I was pretty much dead. I would see people that I served in church with for years, and they would turn and walk the other way. The only church family I had that reached out at this time was Pastor Steve Bubna from the church I was in when I got saved all those years ago. He had someone deliver a used car to us one day and an envelope with almost a thousand dollars in it. He was the only one that showed any support. I remember Jim Baker's son Jay Baker said that the Christian army is the only army that will kill its wounded. That's what was going on. Instead of people reaching out, the church left me to die. Even a call to say they were thinking of me would have been nice.

A few days later, Nena was rushed from her hospital room back to the delivery room with cramps, and once again they couldn't find the babies heart beat. After several hours, they decided to take the baby by C-section. They wheeled Nena back into the surgery room, and they made me wait at the door. It seemed like hours that I waited; I didn't have any fingernails left, and I think I wore a path in the hallway from pacing so much. Finally a nurse came up and said Derrick Junior was in the nursery recoverying and doing fine. My heart was leaping with this news; I took off down the hall to see him. Man Little D was so beautiful. I was so proud to be a daddy to a little handsome man. Nena recovered fine, and they were both out of the hospital in a couple of weeks.

Little Derrick was about four weeks old, and I was the crummiest father in the world. We were down to our last week in the dirty motel before we would have to go back to the house. Nena was on the side of the bed feeding the boy and Jesse was at her friends house. I was laying on the musty smelling cheap motel pastel comforter when the voices started. From each side they hit me. "You piece of shit. You can't and never will be anything. We have told you over and over to stop trying. You are making a fool out of yourself." Then the voice said it. "You would be better off dead, Derrick. If you just kill yourself, they can all move on".

I had a friend named Steve Metsker that once told me that suicide was like a trap door, and once you have decided to kill yourself and step through that door, it's all over. I had stepped through that trap door and had committed to take my own life. I reached over and quietly grabbed my pistol out of the dusty motel nightstand. I got up out of the overly springy bed and knelt over Nena and caressed her head then kissed Little D, then told her I was taking a shower. The steam filled the bathroom and seemed to instantly fogg the mirror as I sat on the toilet and caressed the cold steal in my hand. I asked God to forgive me, and I felt nothing but an empty void as the tears streamed down my face. I wondered if Nena would understand, and then I remember being disgusted that my son would have no memories of me and no stories of me being a decent human. My gag reflex kicked in as I stuffed the barrel of the pistol down my throat; it was cold as the act that I was getting ready to commit. A flash went through my head of Nena screaming and opening the door to see the back of my head and brain matter dripping from the skuzzy wall. With a trembling hand I caressed the trigger as the voices screamed louder saying, "Do it you f'in looser; pull the trigger." Then it happened—a deep breath and a squeeze.

Nothing. This gun had never miss fired one time ever. With a deep breath, I removed the gun. What I didn't feel from God just moments before, I felt now. He showed up and saved my life once again. I removed that bullet to find that the gun fired, but the pin hit just a hair off and didn't ignite the bullet.

I walked out of the bathroom and glanced at Nena still holding little D neither of them having and clue what just unfolded just a few feet from them. "Nena, I'm stepping outside for a few minutes". I watched the cars drive up and down the busy road as I sat on the hood of my car. In the distance, I could hear the roar of tractor trailers on the interstate. My thoughts drifted back to that parking lot where I told God that I was finished. I realized my life had fallen apart because I had not been obedient to his word. Even though I was madly deeply in love with Nena, I had stepped out of the will of God by moving in and sleeping with not only a woman that I wasn't married to, but a women that was still married. We could have done it the right way; we should have done it the right way, but we chose to live by the flesh, and I let God take a back burner to my own desires.

The next day I made some difficult phone calls. I called a deacon at Central that I knew owned a bunch of property, crawled on my belly and begged him to let my family move into the worst house he had. He reluctantly did so with the agreement that I would remodel it while I was there. It was the worst house I had ever lived in. When I cracked open the door the floor moved because of the roaches. There was massive holes in the sheet rock every two feet. The walls had graffiti with massive cartoon penises and all kinds of other lewd art. As bad as that house was, it was a blessing.

I spent hours working on that house—painting, sheet rocking, and cleaning. Nena got a job working home health, so when she was gone, I spent hours praying. It was when the Lakeland revival first started. I would live stream Roy Fields worship and sit in my room and press in. For weeks, I pressed for more, stretching, trying to get my spiritual ears working. Then it happened at once. God said so clearly and so simply. "Start a Church". Wow, No No No you have the wrong guy God, how can I start a church, everyone hates me. "Start a Church", he said again.

Losing It All

From Death to Destiny

CHAPTER TWENTY SEVEN
FRESH START

Fresh Start

I sat at the desk and was mentally and spiritually somewhere in between scared and excited. I decided to give Pastor Honeycutt a call. He answered, and before I had a chance to ask him anything he had a prophetic word of knowledge and said, "Gods telling you to start a church". Wow, how much clear could God be? I expressed to Honeycutt my reservations and he blew my mind with this: "Sometimes God has to make you a zero, so he can be the hero". I had lost everything and was down to being nothing again, so anything that happened would clearly be God making it a success not me.

Two months later, I had come to a settlement on my lawsuit. I paid $680 a month in fines and costs until every dime was paid. It felt good to take responsibility for everything even if the world hated me; I felt good about taking care of it.

First thing was first. Nena's divorce finally went through, so we scheduled the day and got married. Just us, the kids, Big Kenny, and Terry in attendance for the wedding, we were happier than a rat with a cheeto. Finally we were married and right with God. Being right with God felt so good.

Then the pieces started to come together. I knew that God was having me plant a church because I had seen how the body turned on it's own. So that's where I started. I went out and found every person that I knew that had been turned away by the church. We found a building and within a month we were having church in an old bar.

God was moving with in a couple of months we had about fifty people and really developed a great faith community. This was a real training ground for me. Starting a church from the ground up is difficult business. When you're first starting, it's very tempting to just put people in position because you need the help. Bad Idea! I had people doing things that had no business doing them. One of my associate pastors was stepping out on his wife. Another one was drinking in the church office when I wasn't there. The icing on the cake was when we had a women join the church who had the spirit of Jezebel. I watched as she systematically dissected our church. About a year into the church, my rookie mistakes and the Jezzy had tore us apart. What now?

I spent weeks praying asking God the ever so prevalent question, "Why?" One night after crying my eyes out, I heard his voice say very clearly, "I needed you to see what not to do." It turned out that

Fresh Start

this was a training ground. If I could start a church in a place where everyone hated me, then I could start one anywhere, and now I knew all the mistakes that I made and what not to do in moving forward.

During that year, my friends and I some started another band called Blood of Innocence and we quickly were signed to a label and scheduled for tours across the United States. One of the things that the label wanted us to do was move to a bigger city. God kept speaking to me about Kansas City, so it was a easy choice to go. Kansas City, Kansas City here we come.

My cousin Brian called me one day about me planting a church. It was a very strange conversation, since Brian and I had never shared a word about church, God or anything close, ever. He said that his wife's pastor was helping pastors plant churches, and that he felt this inner urge to connect us. Brian, "That's God", I said. He said, "Well, I'm not sure what I think about all that, but I just felt I should connect you." So I drove to Lawrence, Kansas to meet with Justin Miere. It was so comical to see me 6'4" sleeved up with tattoos walk in to his office. I started right out of the gate by saying, "Justin, I have a past and its bad, but I love Jesus. If you can deal with that, let's talk." A month later my entire family moved in with

Justin in Lawrence.

We lived in Lawrence for about a year while we prepared for the Church plant in Kansas City. Kansas City is only thirty minutes from Lawrence so it was a good home base. While in Lawrence, I was a co-pastor of River City Community with Justin. In a meeting one day, Justin and I where brainstorming about a church name. He suggested The Way because that was what the early church was called. It stuck.

Fresh Start

KC Here I Come

Then February of 2010 we moved into the ghetto of Kansas City, Missouri. On a Wednesday and Thursday we had our first gathering in our living room with fifteen people. The Way fellowship was born. That same week I had just gotten a 816 phone number, and I received a phone call from a prophet in New York City. He prophesied over my life for at least thirty minutes about things that only God and I knew. He knew that I didn't trust just anyone, so God told him to prophesy secret things, so I would receive him as a prophet. Then Doug said to me, "I have a word from the Lord. God is going to use you to reopen the prophetic wells of Kansas City." I immediately responded with, "Uhhhh, you got the wrong guy."

Things where getting cramped in our tiny house as we grew and people really wanted to start meeting like a church. We began to look, and wow! I was very ill prepared for what I found. Rent was extremely expensive in the city. Turns out the only place we could find an affordable building was in what are called the West Bottoms. This is a semi abandoned part of town that is desperately trying to make a come back. It's the old stock yards of KC. Every building was built in the 1800's and a lot of gang and mob activity goes on down there especially next to the river because of the easy dumping grounds.

It also is home to five or six haunted houses and the American Royal and Kemper Arena grounds. American Royal is a major attraction for people interested in agriculture and rodeo. Every year it also is home to the National BBQ competition. It also happens to be the place where I came to Jesus.

We moved out of the living room and into our first building in April. It was previously an alternative sex club. We found the forms moving in that you had to sign. A release verifying that you were not law enforcement, media or that you wouldn't file a complaint of any type if you were assaulted. We also had the parking lot with the number one haunted house in the world called the Edge of Hell. It was funny when we would tell people where we were located. "Just north of the Edge of Hell" is what we told them. That was great. It was odd that things had come full circle that I was pastoring a church just a few blocks from where Jesus met me on the floor of that stadium.

During this time was when I had my first angelic encounter. The angel was dressed in white and looked to be a in a male form. He spoke a number to me and said it three times to make sure that it stuck through my unbelief. He said twenty-five thousand, then repeated twenty-five thousand and once again with authority he said twenty-five thousand. The angel then turned walked away and disappeared. Wow! What an amazing experience to have, but what in the world did that mean? I presented it to the congregation and no one knew what it meant. I would later find out exactly who the angel was and roughly what it meant.

Four or five months into the sex club building, we had some bad run-ins with our landlord who apparently practiced witchcraft. He decided that he wanted our praise and worship music pre-approved by him. He went on by saying that he didn't want any hip-hop or any soul type music played because it attracts black people and black people attracts drugs and violence. Well on that note, we started looking for another location.

That week I had my first vision. I showed up to the church to find every single thing that the church owned was missing with no trace of who or where it went. I reached up and took a fist full of hair in each hand beginning to panic. Right then a man that I didn't know appeared in the room and said to me, "Don't worry pastor, we took everything to the new building two blocks from here." In a moment, I found myself at another building where people where putting things together and getting it ready for the church. The man then said, "This is yours to use till you get your own place". Then like a flash I was in a small yard and I had to get all of these orangutans and orange gorillas into the building. So I used corn to lure them in. The gorillas all got in single file and marched into the building. About that time, I heard a thundering or stampeding sound. I turned to see these elephants joyfully frolicking towards us, playing kind of like puppies. I insightfully knew that the elephants were going to trample the gorillas. So I stuck my hands up and said, "STOP NOT YET". And that was it that was the vision.

Sounds all random right?

We could only find one building and guess where it was. Exactly two blocks from where the sex club was. The night I was taking people over to show them, we where stopped by the train that ran in between the two locations and on the train was a RED GORILLA in graffiti art. (And people don't think God speaks to us anymore. God was loud and clear!)

We moved in and God started moving in us. For two years we reached mostly the least of these— a lot of homeless people. We would feed lunch on Friday and serve a small meal on Sunday following service. We also had the privilege of reaching a prison compound that was only four blocks away. It was a release center, so most of the prisoners could leave during the day as long as they checked back in at night. Mighty leaders where raised up out of the ashes of that prison like Rick, who's become my friend and brother. All in all the first two years of ministry we lead at least two thousand people to Jesus.

One strange thing happened during this season. Even though I had witnessed many supernatural things in my life, even with God keeping me alive, I shut down the movement of the Holy Spirit. I had just felt as if charismania had taken things too far, and I lumped it all together and said, "NO."

So by the end of 2012 I was burned out. I couldn't hear God anymore and I was tired and ready to shut the church down. I was spiritually down to nothing, literally spiritually bankrupt. I was laying in bed crying because I couldn't hear God anymore. Little did I know that God had been and still was up to something. Lee Shorter used to always say, "When your down to nothing, God is up to something."

Loud and Clear

I was in the mall one day standing around with my son waiting on my wife and daughter. Two young men kept staring at me from across the corridor. They eventually started walking towards me. I thought, "What in the world do they want?" I had even had the thought come through my mind wondering, "Are they going to pray for me". Then it happened. Josh and Toni descended on me like birds on prey and asked, "Hey man, can we pray for you?" I let them pray, and I had pain in my knee go away. I knew that they were from the IHOP. I could feel it in my spirit. And that day God started to lift the veil off my eyes and let the charismatic and prophetic back in my life.

Within a month we moved across town to a large 65,000 square foot church building. We called it the castle because it was a 1906 built castle looking building. In the first month there, God stretched me beyond what I ever thought possible. The veil would lift more and more everyday. He started to reveal more of my life than I ever thought possible. I had a guy called "The Pilgrim" come by my office with prophetic documents. When reading them, the first thing that I read was a conversation between Bob Jones and one of the other Kansas City Prophets where Bob discussed an angelic encounter he had with Gabriel the arch angel where the angel spoke the number 25,000 to him. As soon as I read that I dropped the paper and knew that God was doing something big with my life.

I received revelation on the vision I had two years before—the one about the gorillas and the elephants. The gorillas were the lost that I was to reach, and the corn was the Word of God. The elephants represented the prophetic movement. I had to stop the prophetic in my life, so I wouldn't skip time and miss what God had planned. The veil was all in Gods plan.

Over the next months we received an average of 150 prophecies a month confirming God was calling me into an apostolic revival mode. One service when we where praying for my wife, a sign and wonder started. Gold dust started to appear. It started on one hand then to both hands then it was all up and down my arms. After that, it was on other people in the congregation. It was great! As the Glory was falling, Joy over took everyone; it was amazing.

One of the craziest manifestations of Heaven that began to happen was when I went to visit a friends church. He had a fine rain that started in his office, like a spiritual mist. Well after that encounter the rain followed me and began to show up in meetings that I was a part of. Additionally, angel feathers and gold dust manifested.

Getting my haircut one day, Jeff Jansen called me on the phone and teold me to get ready because God was getting ready to pour out revival on our church. He said that the Zachariah 4 angel was with me awaking me for the position of revival. That's exactly what had happened. God was awakening me. Six months went by, and I was having daily visions and encounters, prophetic words and every service people would be healed. God was moving through me in a way I didn't even understand. Local prophetic leaders would just stop into services to just be a part of what was going on. In may, of that year Jeff Jansen came and had four meetings with us. We had nearly 300 people and God moved heavily within the group. My wife was healed in that meeting of kidney failure, and I received a new mantel. I received a revivalist mantle.

God reveled to me shortly after those meetings that I had a dual DNA make up. I was apostle and revivalist, or some would say apostle and power evangelist. God is so good; he loves to use us to show his glory.

Eating dinner at a local buffet, God marked a

guy coming in the door. When I say marked, I mean that God would highlight people to me, like a ding in my spirit. The man sat right next to us and within minutes he dropped dead. My wife having a tremendous amount of medical experience and another women ran to help. I picked him up and laid him down on the ground. Several minutes went by as they tried to resuscitate him. The whole time God was screaming at me to raise him from the dead. After Nena and the lady said they where done and his skin was turning gray already, I reached down in faith and screamed "Breath in the name of Jesus!" At that moment the man gasped with a huge breath. God wants us to be dead raisers!

We pressed into the prophetic movement. I received mantels from Jeff Jansen, Phillip Honeycutt, David Hertzog, and Patricia King and then my prophetic anointing jumped up by a thousand when Julie Meyer a talented Prophetess from IHOP prayed over me. Nothing above compared to the mantel that I received at the Divinity Conference. We had Adam F. Thompson and Adrian Beale the authors of The Divinity Code come and do a dream and vision conference at our church. It was a very small turn out probably a little over 100 for the night services, but they were maybe the most powerful services I had ever been a part of in my entire life. God moved in a radical way.

Loud and Clear

A prophet from IHOP named Jess Gjerstad the author of Spiritual Warfare in the End Times, said that the anointing was thick between Adam, Adrian and myself that it reminded him of revivals of the past and the prophecies of the great ones like Bob Jones.

On the last night of meetings at the Divinity Code conference, Adam and Adrian laid there hands on me and said the following. "Derrick, do you know what your name means?" I answered no. And then Adrian said, "Your name is translated 'back to the beginning as the way'". I began to tremble as I felt the anointing begin to drizzle down on me. Heat was over taking my hands and it felt like electricity was shooting through my body. Adam then gave me a word form the Lord, "No matter what you have done in you your life, no matter what people say, you were born for this. You are a catalyst for revival; you are living your destiny." I received the breath of God. Never the same, I was wrecked for God and it is my mission in life to make sure everyone that I meet gets wrecked for him as well.

Since then, we have pursued saving the lost, equipping leaders, hosting the Glory and breathing life into the dead. We just started a Supernatural School where we are raising up a generation of firestarters. We are taking the over the world for Jesus!

It's my prayer that anyone who reads this understands that I'm not trying to glorify myself or even the enemy. I AM trying to glorify my Jesus! Without him, I would NOT be here. If you are struggling in life spiritually, mentally, or even physically, and you don't know the Lord; now is the time to introduce yourself. No matter what you are trying to shove in the hole that's inside of you; if it's drugs, sex, alcohol, or whatever it may be. Remember that the perfect fit for that hole is Jesus Christ! He loves you like no one else could ever love you. His love is perfect and unflawed. He wants so much more for you and your life and chances are you've tried everything else so why not try Jesus? If he can change a wretch like me, then he can change you too. Just step out in faith, all it takes is faith the size of a mustard seed.

Loud and Clear

How do I get saved?

For it is by grace you have been saved, through faith- and this not from yourselves, it is the gift of God- Ephesians 2:8

Grace (salvation) is a gift from God. It is not something you can buy; it is only something you can receive!

For all have sinned and fall short of the glory of God, - Romans 3:23

Every person on this earth has fallen short of what God would want for us. That means that Billy Graham has the same struggles as you do. That also means that those hypocritical Christians that had always thumbed there nose at you have fallen short in the same way. All of our sins are the same.

How do I get Saved?

For the wages of sin is death, but the gift of God is eternal life in Christ Jesus our Lord. – Romans 6:23

This scripture is pretty cut and dry. If you sin without repenting and accepting Christ, the penalty is spiritual death (Hell). If you accept Christ into your heart, you will have eternal life.

In reply, Jesus declared ,"I tell you the truth, no one can see the kingdom of God unless he is born again." – John 3:3

Once again, this is self-explanatory; if you don't have Jesus in you life, you don't go to heaven, and we all know what the alternative is, don't we.

That if you confess with your mouth, "Jesus is Lord," and believe in your heart that God raised him from the dead, you will be saved. For it is with your heart that you believe and are justified, and it is with your mouth that you confess and are saved. – Romans 10: 9 & 10

So let me ask you:

Are you a sinner?

Do you want forgiveness for your sins?

Do you believe Jesus died on the cross for you and rose again?

Are you willing to surrender your life to Christ?

Are you ready to invite Jesus into your heart and into your life right now where you are?

If you have answered yes to these, say this prayer right now where you are. You don't have to say it out loud or make it super holy or reverent. God wants to meet you right where you are—right this second!

Prayer: Lord, I have sinned against you. I want forgiveness for all my sins. I believe that Jesus died on the cross for me and rose again. Father, I give you my life to do with as you wish. I want Jesus Christ to come into my life and into my heart this very second in Jesus name. Amen.

How do I get Saved?

It is very important for you to know this very minute the devil will try to convince you that your not good enough or that this is all fake or that you can never make it as a Christian. You tell that scumbag that he is a liar and he has to leave RIGHT NOW in the name of JESUS!

Keep in the word! Faith cometh by hearing and hearing cometh by the word of God!

Be blessed and highly favored by our Lord Jesus Christ!

Pastor Derrick Gates

From Death to Destiny

Bible Verses to study

The thief comes only to steal and kill and destroy; I have come that they may have life, and have it to the full. – John 10:10

"They overcame him by the blood of the Lamb and by the word of their testimony" – Revelation 12:11

If then, though you are evil, know how to give good gifts to your children, how much more will your Father in heaven give the Holy Spirit to those who ask him!"

– Luke 11:13

And I will ask the Father, and he will give you another counselor to be with you forever – John 14:16

"I baptize you with water for repentance. But after me will come one who is more powerful than I, whose sandals I am not fit to carry. He will baptize you with the Holy Spirit and with fire. – Matthew 3:11

How do I get Saved?

And these signs will accompany those who believe: in my name they will drive out demons; they will speak in new tongues; -Mark 16:17

On one occasion, while he was eating with them , he gave them this command: "do not leave Jerusalem, but wait for the gift my Father promised, which you have heard me speak about. For john baptized with water, but in a few day you will be baptized with the Holy Spirit." – Acts 1:4,5

But you will receive power when the Holy Spirit comes on you; and you will be my witnesses in Jerusalem, and in all Judea and Samara and to the ends of the earth." – Acts 1:8

All of them were filled with the Holy Spirit and began to speak in other tongues as the Spirit enabled them. – Acts 2:4

Be Joyful always; pray continually; give thanks in all circumstances, for this is Gods will for you in Christ Jesus

- 1 Thessalonians 5:17

Rejoice evermore. Pray without ceasing. In every thing give thanks: for this is the will of God in Christ Jesus concerning you.

- 1 Thessalonians 5:16-18

"the Spirit of the Lord is on me, because he has anointed me to preach good news to the poor. He has sent me to proclaim freedom for the prisoners and recovery of sight for the blind, to release the oppressed, to proclaim the year of the Lord's favor."

– Luke 4:18, 19

For Gods gifts and his call are irrevocable. – Romans 11:29

He said to them, "Go into all the world and preach the good news to all creation. - Mark 16:15

"Do not judge, or you too will be judged. For in the same way you judge others, you will be judged, and with the measure you use, it will be measured to you.- Matthew 7:1-2

"Why do you look at the speck of sawdust in your

How do I get Saved?

brother's eye and pay no attention to the plank in your own eye? - Matthew 7:3

"The King will reply, 'I tell you the truth whatever you did for one of the least of these brothers of mine, you did for me.' - Matthew 25:40

Made in the USA
Monee, IL
13 September 2021